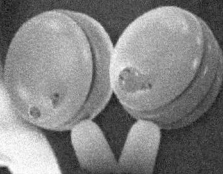

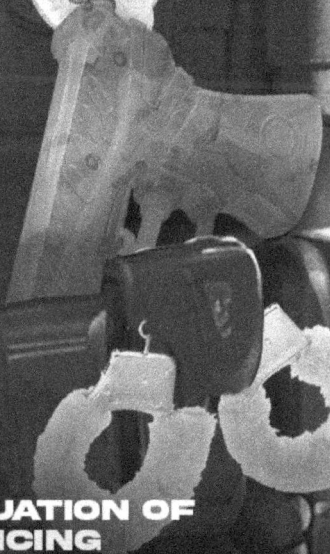

ISBN: 979-8-9872564-7-3

DEDICATIONS

To everyone, I appreciate you picking this book up.
Thank you for your interest in reading it.
It means the world to me.

To my wife and two daughters, your love, patience, and guidance
over the past 45 years have made me a better person.
Thank you from the bottom of my heart.

To my brothers and sisters in law enforcement,
Thank you.

Seen through the eyes of a seasoned, mid-western big city cop, Steve Wickelgren gives you a real-life perspective on the welcomed and often forced transformation of policing in our nation; how it has evolved- the good, the bad and the ugly, and how if we as a nation don't recognize the even uglier direction we are headed; bad laws put into play by liberal politicians, lowered values and personal responsibility, and the lack of accountability by our courts, God knows what our society and the "next" evolution in modern day policing will look like.

—SHERIFF ERNEST L. BEITEL III, RETIRED

TABLE OF CONTENTS

NOTE FROM THE AUTHOR

I want you to know why I decided to share my experience and observations with the world. I am a bit of an introvert. I have spent most of my life looking at what others are doing, paying attention to them, and studying them, wondering what they are doing and why.

I now see myself as a closet sociologist of sorts. Over the years, I have also often pushed myself into things I wasn't comfortable with, and becoming a cop was one. Teaching cops was another.

Taking the assignment as our department counselor and attending graduate school to be licensed as a therapist was another big one. I pushed myself out of my introversion but will forever be an introvert.

My goal is to help people see the desire and struggles law enforcement goes through. I want people to see that these people working in the profession are well-meaning, flawed, dedicated, sometimes wrong, and human. I want people to understand that they make mistakes, but they make mistakes at the same rate that everyone makes mistakes. No one is perfect, and no one will ever be perfect because we are human. Cops can do better. People can do better. If encounters with law enforcement keep worsening, I will guess it's generally because the people are getting worse. Let's understand the job of a law enforcement officer before we judge them. I hope this book will show what I believe to be the main reasons why we have arrived where we are with society's attitude toward the profession.

Intro

I'M SITTING DOWN WITH ONE OF MY CLIENTS, who just happened to be a law enforcement officer (LEO), for a session. I remember discussing the exact details of a 911 call and the officer's brain response. I found myself doing this often when I was getting to the end of nearly 27 years in law enforcement. They'd come to me for various reasons, to discuss a traumatic shooting, family problems, PTSD, anxiety, you name it. I became an LEO counselor because I wanted to help, give back, and introduce a psychological conversation about police encounters. After working the job for 15 years, it was an honor to start helping these folks. Most people don't know what goes on in the brain during a police encounter between an officer and a civilian.

That's a loaded topic. There's a lot that's going on there. I want to unpack this conversation with you in this book. I want to show you what police encounters look like from a law enforcement officer's perspective. In addition, there are very real cultural challenges that affect how we see the world and associate ourselves with Society. I want to reintroduce an old conversation about the fabric of our culture and how it helps us or hurts us in life. The fabric of who we are impacts everything we do, think, and feel in life, so it's a big conversation. A conversation I feel uniquely qualified to discuss with you. I don't think I know all the answers about how to fix today's polarizing environments surrounding policing. However, I'd like to see if I can improve our understanding of policing.

Perhaps I can incorporate a new perspective that's not currently in Society's conversation. I feel it's been around for a while but maybe it is under-communicated. A perspective that sees the value in our institutions and recognizes elements that serve those institutions to keep them going in the right direction. Also, one that's not afraid to point out some areas that undermine the things we care about.

I imagine I've already stepped on some people's toes, and we're only three paragraphs into this thing. That's not necessarily my intention, but I know it will happen. Many things contribute to areas of contention in politics, media, culture, and technology that affect lives in meaningful ways. What should we do about them? How should we allow these things to affect our lives? We'll look at some of these pivotal areas of the domain and see how they contribute to our lack of understanding, increased violence, and racism.

I often ask myself something like, what happened that took us away from some sense of harmony in policing? Obviously, there is no singular answer but a call for an inquiry. What are the cops doing differently to cause such an uproar in Society? Or, how is Society approaching the conversation and understanding of policing? I realize there was a significant change on both fronts. From a lack of training, police officers may or may not be aware of mental illness in a police confrontation.

On the other hand, if Society has disregarded the role of modern-day policing then that is a huge problem. These are some fundamental issues that are worth discussing. Because of this breakdown, people's lives are affected. Unlike any other industry, when policing goes wrong, either at the officer's or the civilian's fault, it has deep and lasting consequences. In some cases, life-changing consequences.

Why in the world would a cop shoot someone? Most people don't have an answer to that question. Even though we see a story every other day in the news about a police shooting, most of Society is unaware of all the elements that go into something like that. I don't take this conversation lightly. I remember an incident when I had to pull my gun out on a call. That call echoed in my mind for 25 years before I finally felt I had some resolve. Should I take the shot? I'm looking at the suspect holding a gun to someone else's head. Should I take the shot? In a matter of split seconds, I'm thinking about my family, my partner, my training, and the victim. If I don't take the shot then my family would be attending my funeral. Or if I did, I'd be in the paper and in the courts. What should I do? That call left moderate effects on my brain that produced symptoms and would likely continue to do so had I not addressed that incident directly, although it was addressed 25 years later.

It's situations like that that happen daily in America and worldwide. That call changed my life. That stayed with me in considering how I can help people in police encounters. How can we help the cops? How can we help civilians? There are real practical things that we can do and be aware of that could increase the likelihood of good outcomes amid bad situations.

I want to stoke a conversation of informed intrigue around policing. Like, What defines a good cop versus a bad cop? How much training is essential for police officers to do their work? What goes into the backstory of policing? What should we expect from police officers? What are they hired to do? Let's look at the 30,000-foot view and hopefully find some light at the end of the tunnel. You are worth it; your community and your city are worth it. Thanks for having this conversation with me. I think we'll both get a lot out of it.

CHAPTER 1

The Breakdown

TODAY, A POLICE SHOOTING CAN HAPPEN AT 11:05 A.M., and it's broadcasted on social media live-streamed in real-time. At 11:35 a.m., it's sent worldwide through news notifications on people's devices. The preceding days and weeks can be a centralized forum for opinions, theories, political narratives, and plenty of emotions. Everybody gets to develop their summary judgments about what went wrong. I often ask myself what other industries are like this? With law enforcement, there is an instantaneous craze when it comes to reporting encounters.

I get it; it is emotionally charging. An ordinary person is going about their day, and boom, there is an article on their phone about somebody stealing something at the local mall and getting shot on the way out. Nothing about that is normal, and it's so extreme that we're hooked on it. We got to find out everything that we need to know about this. Is our life under threat because of this situation? People think, this is my local mall; is it safe to go in there now? I want to read the article to find out whose fault it is. I mean, someone got shot. People need to be held accountable if they're going to shoot someone.

It's easy to fill in the blank with your most recent police-involved shooting or brutality story. Everyone has a new one broadcasted to them each week by their favorite media outlet. The New York Times has a special section where you can check up on the trending police brutality stories around the globe. No other line of work has this instantaneous craze for attention. Anytime something like this is reported, it's considered extreme because it is extreme. On a typical day for an average person, things aren't stolen, and people aren't shot or taken to jail. Anytime there's a confrontation with authority, there could be less desirable and bad outcomes. Sometimes, those confrontations don't go very well. When they don't, everybody knows about it, and the opinions mount. Some people say cops should go to jail for shooting someone who stole something so small. Others say cops shouldn't be allowed to have guns. The suspect should have been just given a ticket. They're even saying people should be able to steal from corporations because they make so much money. Everyone has their perspective and their opinion, and that is their right.

What about the officer? Were they doing the right thing? Are they a good cop or a bad cop? Maybe all police officers are monsters! We should defund them and disband all police departments. Do we even need them anymore? It's evident that society has introduced new conversations to challenge the narrative that police officers are to be trusted because they are here to serve us. Instead, an ever-growing narrative of innocent person vs. bad cop is being conveyed as the common police encounter. How did society go from the harmony of acceptance in law enforcement into believing they are actually the primary problem?

Conversations like this and, more recently, conversations that include such stark criticisms of the police department have been more prevalent. These are some big subjects, and I will approach some aspects of the bigger conversation in each chapter. I plan to break down the complexity surrounding these encounters. I'm not going to approach this book as a way to convince you to only see it through a policeman's lens; we're going to look at every angle.

Obviously, I was a police officer, and I will share with you the perspective of a law enforcement officer. My perspective may shed some misconceptions and enlighten you about their training, politics in policing, the officer's mental state, the human side of policing, and the appropriate response to police encounters.

I'm also going to tackle the elements that go into a police encounter from the side of the civilian. What are they bringing into the encounter? What kind of emotions would they typically be emitting? What are they culturally inclined to do in these kinds of situations? When confronted by law enforcement, does their brain tell them to fight, run, or freeze? What are their rights, and how do they make it through police encounters alive?

The third contribution is a conglomerate of external factors that contribute to the underpinnings of our society, politics, technology, and media. I want to show you how our society can affect us positively and negatively, especially concerning police encounters. We'll also look at how technology can benefit these interactions and also how it can hinder them. We're going to talk about the media, its propensities towards negativity bias, and how that drives our brain to look for certain things. These factors build the foundation of our thoughts and feelings about police interactions. They are very big subjects and will take some time to unpack, so bear with me as I try to guide you down a journey of my past. I want you to glean from my perspective to gain new ways to think about our present-day problems.

I MADE THE PAPER

I grew up in the south Chicago suburbs bordering the city and was exposed to a lot of diversity and culture. In 1966 I was in kindergarten, and one of the prominent newspapers at the time was reporting from our school. They snapped a picture of me walking on the sidewalk where the buses were alongside one of the first black kids allowed to go to our school. The classes of students before me didn't have any black kids in them. I remember the picture clear as day; it is cemented in my mind as an important moment. My three older brothers didn't have black kids in their class. Imagine that dichotomy, it was customary for me to go to school with them, but to my brothers, it wasn't.

I was exposed to cultural diversity since I was in kindergarten; it was a normal part of life. When I moved to Minnesota with my family, I realized it wasn't normal for everyone. There is definitely a little bit of culture shock. We were in a tiny rural town that received an exchange student here and there, but it was void of any cultural mixing. Seeing those two worlds at a young age opened up my mind to have different thoughts about people. I've always liked the diversity. You get to see the world from everybody's perspective and experiences. It was balancing, in some way, emotionally.

My upbringing shaped my perspective and has assisted my

view of the world. My parents taught me that you should be good to people and treat others as you would want to be treated. They got me thinking a lot about other people. I became fascinated as a teenager with psychology. It was the only magazine I subscribed to. Other kids would read comic book magazines, and I'm reading about behavioral interactions and brain function. I got excited about potentially doing something where I could be paid to "think," which would be my career.

I still did dumb things just like any other kid would. I remember walking to a local convenience store with my friends one day when I was nine. I saw that the cement curb was just poured, and it was soft. So we thought it'd be fun to put our footprints in it and leave our mark. It was a five-and-dime candy store. Just as we were putting our feet prints in this wet cement, the people that just finished the job drove by. They slammed on the brakes, got out and grabbed us, and called the cops. Now I'm sitting in the back of a cop car, scared shitless; I was so scared I thought I might die. The cop asked me for my address, and I had no idea what my address was. He asked me for my phone number, and I was able to remember that.

I knew I'd messed up big, and my dad would be so mad. I wasn't scared that a cop would beat me up or something. I knew the actual punishment was going to come at home. My parents raised me to see cops as the ultimate authority in our lives. They hold people accountable and catch the bad guys while helping the good ones. I knew if I called 911, they'd be there to help me if there was an emergency. They were an authority figure. Like in school when the principal says you've been messing up in class. They would bring out the rulers and hangers, and you would get swatted, spanked, slapped, and beaten up if you didn't behave.

We always knew not to mess around in school because the principal would call my parents, and the punishment that I got would continue at home. I don't necessarily agree with beating kids up in school without the parent's permission as an effective means of learning, but I got the point. I was to be accountable for my own actions, and that was my lesson. This was a mindset that I carried for the rest of my life. If somebody's acting out, there should be someone there to hold them accountable to keep harmony and peace so that everybody can go on with their lives.

I BECAME A LEO

I had a roommate going into law enforcement, and I was fascinated with what he shared with me. There's a class that I could take to help me out with my four-year degree in sociology, and it just hooked me. I knew there would be a variety in life if I pursued a career in law enforcement. One moment could be report writing, the next chasing criminals, the next moment eating donuts. Whatever it was, I knew I could interact with people and use my fascination with understanding people's thoughts, actions, emotions, and behavior to do some good.

I became licensed as a police officer in 1986, working most of my years as a cop with the Minneapolis Police Department. I had an absolutely wonderful career with Minneapolis. I worked the street, administrative assignments, training, investigations, promotion to Sergeant, and most uniquely, an assignment for my last 13 years running the Employee Assistance Program. In that position, I received my Master's degree in counseling and became licensed as a Marriage & Family therapist.

I was signing up to serve people. I swore to uphold the constitution and the laws of the land. I was there to protect people from career criminals and bad actors. When I say bad actors, I don't mean the Kardashians; I'm talking about people out there to harm others. In my career, I worked in many different areas of law enforcement. I initially started in a small town. It was so small that we sometimes only received three or four calls weekly. The captain would tell us to stack up our civilian encounters so we could record them to make sure they got the political clout with how busy we were. Because the town was so small, everybody knew everybody. I would practically go make chess appointments with a local barber to consider it a civilian encounter and report it on my daily activities log. We would make it look like we're busy to justify earning a paycheck. It was typical government functions at its finest. Every year the city sets a budget for the police department, and you need to use it to keep it. Every year you've got to convince the budget committee that you need more money this year and hope they give it to you. No wonder why some cops got caught by the local reporters sleeping in the movie theater on duty.

I'm more of a bigger city kind of person, so when I got the chance to join things in Minneapolis, that's where my career developed. I have had many assignments through the years. I did a lot of classic police work. One of my favorite assignments was when I was a part of the research and development unit. The military was selling helicopters to the government or agencies for a dollar. I was tasked with researching the possibility of purchasing these helicopters to piece one together so the Departments could use them. We would buy six of them in the hopes that we would get one good one that we could use.

I also did some organized crime work and had a short stint in the narcotics unit. I was on something called the city-wide crack team. Yeah, it's called the city-wide crack team. We would look for plumbers' crack, site it, and ticket it to keep those mooner landings at bay. Naa, we were looking for another crack, crack cocaine. Cocaine was a very big problem then.

Every day I would suit up and chase career criminals for many years. Some people had outstanding warrants and suspects that we were on to regarding their criminal activity. These guys were serious criminals. Their 9 to 5 job was to break the law and harm as many people as possible doing whatever illegal thing they wanted. Some of them were huge in identity theft and credit card fraud. Others were big into drugs and gang violence. Most of the time I was a plainclothes officer, and I used an unmarked car to do a lot of surveillance.

At any given time, I would research about five or six suspects on my team, track their whereabouts, and wait for them to commit a crime. One of the targets I was assigned was a nighttime burglar, so I would sit at his house, wait for him to leave, and follow him to a potential victim's home. Another target loved doing airport runs to pickpocket people coming off an international flight. He believed that the wealthier people with higher credit card limits were flying internationally, so he would always wait by the international terminals. So, I'd follow him around town, and I'd only get excited when he'd make a trip to the airport. I called my team once he was headed to the airport, and they would come and support me with our potential arrest.

We also did a lot of work around the prostitution parlors.

There were special massage parlors that were illegal. The prostitutes, or what they call themselves, the massage therapists, had a long history of getting arrested for such work. A person soliciting their services would go in and go through some detector to see if they're wearing a wire. Then they would get undressed and pay for prostitution. As a plainclothes officer, my colleagues would make an appointment and go through all the transaction steps to bust the prostitute in action. They'd make it through the wire detectors, and then they would turn their mic on. We would all listen in and wait for the bust word to be said, and then conduct The Sting. We take a ram and bust the door down and make the arrests. I remember my Sergeant used to tell me, "Hey, Steve, you're going to be the next one to go in." I knew what that meant; I would have to go in there, get undressed, and wait for the bust to happen. I always responded, Respectfully, "F*** you". We'd have a good laugh about it. We enjoyed making arrests that we felt helped clean up the neighborhoods and the communities.

I did a lot of other police work that I'll share later in the book, but hopefully, you can glean a little bit from my history and perspective. I transitioned from being a law enforcement officer to a counselor for the department. I knew when I saw the position open up that I was interested. On the one hand, I'd never be able to return to being a standard officer with the department because taking this position puts me in an elevated state with the department. I'd be meeting with people regularly, talking about their most personal problems along with their families. I'd be more of an island department because you can't have your counselor come back in as your peer after they hear all your dirt. I knew it would be a challenging, yet very helpful role. So I decided to take the plunge, and I went back to school, finished up my master's, and took the job. I've been helping people individually for years, teaching the department different pieces of training.

That transition allowed me to think from an elevated standpoint about how to help my community. I also learned how to help law enforcement officers and everything they have to go through and deal with daily. I learned more about how law enforcement families face the challenges that they have been part of, with something like a law enforcement career. Most of all, I started seeing things from a third-person perspective. Having been in a law enforcement career and being a part of a community, I could see how people respond to different policing situations and how it affects them. This allowed me to approach the big issues of today from an unbiased standpoint. I started to think about the areas where policing could be improved and where it's lacking. Simultaneously, fatherlessness in a community sets up a detrimental path for the kids. Across the board, I started addressing these situations individually with the families that would come to me. Still, I realized these were the same problems happening across the country.

THE TURNING POINT

At the end of my time in law enforcement, when I transitioned fully to counseling, I noticed a breakdown in sentiment. The tide morphed and changed culturally to something far removed from where it was. The political environment was so charged that you couldn't hear your own thoughts about a situation;

you could only hear the thoughts coming from your designated party. In many cases, it felt like the facts didn't matter anymore. I remember one politician specifically saying that facts don't matter; we have to push our agenda.

It's easy to feel overwhelmed by the uncertainty that surrounds policing and how it's viewed. It feels like there are more questions than answers sometimes. As I discussed this topic with many people, the feedback I receive is that they're unaware of the solutions. They're only given a perspective from their left or right-leaning media outlets or a snippet of online interaction void of any context and due process.

What level of accountability does the officer have, and how much accountability does the civilian need to accept? There should be some standards, right? Standards allow us to set the bar high to achieve it and be mindful when we miss the mark. Are cops allowed to make mistakes on the job just as anyone else is allowed to make mistakes in their profession? Let's get to the bottom of these questions to find reasonable answers.

I've also noticed clearly visible severe cultural norms that cloud people's ability to behave in a socially acceptable way. Some very strong underpinnings in the family unit help a child grow up and know which way they should go or severely hinder a child. Our culture should assist our ability to grow and flourish in our community. However, some cultures allow disruptive, destructive behaviors that introduce hate, anger, and violence, leading to more bad situations.

After spending several decades in law enforcement and transitioning to counseling people in law enforcement, the equilibrium of policing is off. Society's perspective on policing is off. This led to a breakdown in harmony. On both sides of the badge, people are getting hurt needlessly. We face these fundamental problems, and we need to find answers to them. Let's work together to become enlightened individually and as a community.

CHAPTER 2

Eyes Of The Officer

MY PARTNER AND I GOT A CALL FOR SERVICE ABOUT A GUY that was said to be intoxicated. We showed up, and he showed visible signs of intoxication. He passed out drunk on someone's porch. He was lying flat on his back with his eyes closed. You can smell alcohol on his breath, and he was snoring. We tried to wake him by rubbing his chest and talking to him. "Hey, hey, wake up, wake up!" He was not very responsive, and two paramedics showed up around that time. The paramedics assisted us in getting him up off the ground, and we kept trying to wake him up. "Hey, come on, wake up." He finally sits up and starts pulling away from us. Then he started to get violent. My partner started doing a wrist lock on him to control him. The medics begin assisting us in his struggle. As we commenced wrestling him for control, one of the medics saw something, ran behind the guy, grabbed his shirt on his back, and pulled it up almost over his head. The medic then starts screaming at us to lay him down. It turns out someone stabbed him in the back with an ice pick three times.

He had two collapsed lungs, and I realized, Oh my God, he wasn't just a drunk guy fighting us; he was literally fighting for his life. I really felt bad for that guy. It was a huge lesson in learning situational awareness. Every person you encounter is different, and it could be dealing with something that impairs their judgment and ability to communicate. In this situation, his behavior was alarming, and we thought he was getting violent; ultimately, he was fighting for his life because of his wounds.

After I started working in the mental health field, one of the core principles I learned was perspective. Perspective gives us the ability to see not only our thoughts in a different light as a third person, looking at our thoughts individually and sorting them appropriately, but it gives us the ability to see what other people are seeing regarding the same situations. Seeing the world through someone else's eyes is extremely enlightening, and there's so much to learn.

In the process of truth and transparency, it would be appropriate to share the perspective of police officers. What does the world look like through the eyes of an officer? Not very many people know what that world looks like. As I share, this perspective is not to discount anyone else's perspective. I hope to start a conversation rather than make absolutes about right and wrong. I hope to shed some light on my experience and how it could be helpful to the community. I want to bring everybody closer, so we can get to the heart of the crucial matters and not be so divisive. I ask for you to suspend your judgment for a short while to entertain a new perspective. I think it's extremely valuable to hear all sides of an argument to render any conclusions. So, regardless of your fundamental beliefs or political affiliations, try to see the helpful side in my dialogue.

POLICE WORK IS NOT PRETTY

Have you ever been to a baseball game? A common thing you do at a baseball game is get a hot dog, put some ketchup and mustard and a little relish on it, and enjoy. It tastes good and feels nostalgic in some ways, relating to an American pastime. What we don't want to see and experience is what goes into making that hot dog. It could be pigs' ass cheeks and intestines, among other not-so-pleasant things to talk about. It's not pleasant to see the process of making hot dogs, either. It makes most of us uncomfortable, similar to garbage collecting. We all need our garbage collected, but we'd rather not think about how that happens or the gross smells and visuals that garbage collectors have to deal with. We'd prefer to wrap our trash in beautiful plastic bags and throw them in a plastic bin and have somebody else take care of the rest. Police work can be perceived as collecting trash and cleaning up the city or the process of making the things we enjoy. We would wholeheartedly request that we are never shown the process; just give us the end result with a bow tie.

Why is it so unpleasant? The nature of the job is to enforce a level of compliance with the laws of the land. Those laws were put in place by elected officials, by the people to shape and develop what is to be considered acceptable behaviors in public. We have speed limits because people decided that certain speeds were not acceptable in certain areas for safety concerns. Laws were enacted around acceptable behaviors within your household. They're there to protect you and your family members from socially unacceptable behaviors. There seems to be a growing list of unacceptable behaviors, but I'll cover a few. Certain drugs are against the law to have in your possession and to consume. Either those drugs are harmful to you or could be potentially harmful to the community, so much so that there was a law in place to police them.

Another example is battery; physically assaulting someone, in most cases, is against the law. Obviously, there are very important areas of self-defense, but the bottom line is that you are not allowed to assault people physically. It's not good for you, and it's definitely not good for the person you're physically assaulting. Some laws pertain to the home, and laws are specific to the streets and the communities, while other laws are set aside specifically for individuals and their rights. The laws do differ greatly based on where you live, and the enforcement of those laws is up to the local jurisdiction.

In some cases, laws are up for interpretation. The interpretation is conveyed to the officers on duty through the lens of their local law enforcement departments. That interpretation is then subjected to legal counsel and regularly brought before the court of the land. Many factors go into the interpretation of said laws, which I will get into later in the book. Nevertheless, the officers are enacted to enforce the laws and let the courts render judgments and verdicts.

In essence, police officers receive a menu of the laws of their land and go about their day or go on service calls to enforce them. Police officers aren't magical unicorns. Some people expect them to be top-grade lawyers, social workers, and law enforcement officers all in one. That's just not the case, and it may never be. In big cities where there might be more officers on duty, they can receive more training based on funding. In small cities with fewer officers on duty and less funding, they might receive less training. Lawyers go through several years of law school to understand a niche within the law and practice it regularly. The amount of law that a typical officer receives is and can be basic to enforce common law regularly. There is really no expectation for police officers to know every law but a hopeful expectation that as the officers proceed through their training into years of experience, they will receive more training on how to do their job better. In small cities, police officers might not be able to receive additional training, which is a real problem.

Police officers must conduct these unpleasant encounters in a glass bowl. Everyone is watching all the time and judging what you say, look like, and act every second of every day. On most occasions, cops are recorded as well, so someone else can review your behavior. What other profession carries such transparency when every encounter is recorded and potentially reviewed in a court of law?

WHAT ARE POLICE OFFICERS SUPPOSED TO DO ON A SERVICE CALL?

What is the worst possible thing you could do right now? That's what police calls are filled with every single day. Police typically encounter people in their worst possible state. 911 calls don't start with perfect dates and walks on the beach to check out the sunset. Cops find people in the worst possible state in their lives. Whether they're in the middle of a scuffle and they're fighting someone or they're in the middle of doing an illegal activity. They're stealing or hurting someone. They could be in the middle of an emergency or completely intoxicated. Cops are the ones that meet them in these terrible moments in their life and assess the help that's needed.

Once a call for service goes out through someone initiating a 911 call, the responding officers may receive some assessment information before the call, and sometimes they don't get any. The officers must then show up on the scene and be prepared for several scenarios. Based on the call, they determined some level of readiness. The severity and weight of the disturbance will warrant a heightened and more forceful response.

Once they arrive, the officer has various methods to determine the necessary course of action. They show up on the scene ready to encounter any civilian, and they have to put together a rapid assessment of facts. The officer will use their training, emotional regulation, and knowledge coming into the call. They will assess who is on the other side of the call for service or investigation as a civilian. Are they a suspect in the investigation? If so, who's the suspect? What's going on in their mind? Are they going to harm themselves? Are they going to harm the police officer? Are they mentally unstable? Have they had any prior police interactions? Is this your first time dealing with a police officer, or do they have prior convictions? What kind of behavior were they displaying before, during, and after the police interaction? Were they breaking any of the laws? What would a judge say about the encounter if considered in a court of law? The officer goes through a series of steps to dispel threats and suspicions and to conclude lawful and acceptable behavior or what actions are needed to satisfy the encounter.

In big cities, police officers go from one call to the next. They may finish a call where they are taking someone in for domestic disturbance or driving under the influence, and they get a call to help out with a possible overdose. Each call they receive presents them with a whole host of new variables that they need to take into account and bring about public peace through their situational awareness.

The officer will likely be equipped with a partner and various tools at their disposal, including body cam, lethal and non-lethal weapons. The officer's most important tool is their training, demeanor, emotional awareness, and ability to diffuse conflict to find helpful resolutions. Of course, an officer has at their disposal their strong and forceful responses if absolutely necessary to save lives. The strong and forceful response, however, is not required or necessary in the majority of police encounters.

In a matter of seconds, the officers need to assess the situation and come to very fast resolutions in some encounters. If they pull someone over for speeding and the driver jumps out of the car and aggressively pursues the police officer's vehicle with something in their hand that looks like a weapon, then the officer needs to make very fast decisions on what to do. The officers are always assessing the threat level to themselves, the environment, and the individuals they're speaking to. No other industry continually runs into this type of constant conflict under the threat of personal bodily harm.

These situations have varying degrees of complexity, and no two calls of service are alike. The people they will be encountering are different, and their mindsets about the laws in the land are different. Their perspective on law enforcement is different. Their mental state is different. Every single police call for service is different from the last. The only thing that can be somewhat consistent is the officer's ability to respond and utilize their training in order to bring about the best possible solutions.

Emotions are extraordinarily high in police encounters. Regardless of the call for service, when stopped by law enforcement in any investigatory manner, people's right to movement may be restricted and halted. People may be detained temporarily while an investigation is underway. There is a period of limbo where the officer investigates something, and compliance is requested and sometimes required from the civilian. This halting of free motion, where the civilian is not allowed to leave unless the investigation is concluded, can be very alarming and troubling to individuals. In some cases, people's emotional response brings them to a state of alarm where they want to fight or flight, which is to run away, or freeze.

The officer has emotions that are surging as well during these encounters. The officer and civilian both have two primary cognitive drivers for their ability to respond. The limbic system in our brain deals with the emotional center, which may tell us to run from conflicts. On the other hand it may want us to stay and fight because of our desire to help, much like military combat soldiers. In large part, we have one side of the brain: the logical side. On the other side of their brain, is their emotional response. Without going into too much detail on the brain's function, the emotional side sometimes shuts down our ability to think logically. When we feel threatened, we feel anxious and powerless and react based on those feelings rather than thinking logically about what to do. The officer does have the training to better manage the natural emotional response and proceed with their training response. This is most evident in situations where there's an emergency like a fire, and officers and the fire department run into the fire to save people when everyone else's emotional response tells them to run away from the fire. The same goes into effect when people are shooting a gun in public, and the officers run towards the gunfire when everyone else runs away. Good officers learn how to regulate their emotions in every situation.

ACTION BEATS REACTION

Dr. Bill Lewinski was one of my professors in the early 80s. He developed The Force Institute. He did several studies similar to the concept of action beats reaction. One study he did was from an officer-involved shooting in Minneapolis. Minneapolis had an incident where someone was running away from the cops with a gun, turned around as he was running, pointed the gun back at the cop, and fired a round or two. The police officer saw that person turning and saw the gun. They were being fired upon and decided to shoot back. By the time the officer fired back, the person had already turned back around as he was running away. Everyone was upset because they said he was just trying to escape. The mean cop shot him in the back. When interviewed, the cop said he was facing me when I fired back. So, Dr. Lewinsky did studies about how long it takes the brain to see the threat and make a decision. The conclusion of the study showed that a person can turn around quicker than the brain can react to a decision to shoot and then actually shoot. It is similar to the research regarding action always beats reaction. If you are trying to respond to someone's action, you will not have enough time to respond, thus making the situation more difficult to assess. In situations like this, the cop must assess whether deadly force is necessary. The most basic description of deadly force is whether I or someone else is about to seriously get hurt or killed; if so, I need to stop that threat.

When you recognize a threat, you have to decide how to stop that threat. Is it safe to do so? Because if I'm shooting my gun, will I hit another person if I miss the suspect? Is there someone else that could get hurt? And all of this decision-making happens in a second or two. That's a quick decision, and sometimes a second is all it takes to make the wrong one, and nobody is perfect.

ASK, TELL, MAKE

My policing was not perfected at home. Believe me, ask, tell, make doesn't work on your daughters. It goes against healthy relational dynamics. I learned that the hard way. It only works on criminals and people resisting lawful orders. I spent my days dealing with violent criminals and trained my brain to defuse the behavior that could harm us or the people around us. Every police call was a call to stop the bad behavior. I had developed this deep-seated fear that if my family didn't listen to me, they could turn into these scumbag criminals I see daily. If one of my daughters doesn't brush their teeth right, then they will be on the fast track to becoming a gang member. Of course, that was not rational, and I sought therapy for it. I just wanted the best for them and was trained to stop the bad behaviors. We all have the ability to address our irrational fears and work on ourselves so we see the world as it is, not as our fears predict it to be.

The civilian is generally requested to change their behavior if deemed inappropriate. This could mean a wide variety of things. I went to calls all the time where people were in apartment buildings, and a husband and wife were fighting, yelling at the top of their lungs. The call for service requested a well-being check to be conducted on their building because it sounded like someone was getting murdered. We would show up and see if anyone needed assistance and enforce the local ordinances.

Generally, good officers operate from a framework of ask, tell, and then make. The progression of ask, tell, and make is a structure that allows the civilian to comply with the officer's lawful request. They are given a command that the officer believes is lawful. That command is a request for compliance. The civilian has to obey a lawful command from the police officer. If the officer doesn't receive compliance, then the officer will proceed to tell the civilian to cooperate. If that doesn't work, then the officer will escalate the encounter to make them obey, which sometimes goes into physical restraints, handcuffs, sitting in the back of the patrol car, and various forms of physical control.

This progression of obedience requested through this lawful encounter does not feel comfortable in any way. Sometimes people are requested to exit their vehicles when they're stopped for speeding. Sometimes people are requested to stop in the middle of their day when they're running late to work. Sometimes people are stopped in the supermarket when they're peacefully shopping. These encounters can seem abrupt and intrusive. It's not the nature of the police officer to make it more uncomfortable than necessary. It's the officer's job to satisfy the call for service or investigate suspicious behavior.

If you are under arrest, the officer will ask you to cooperate. Can you turn around and put your hands behind your back? I will handcuff you now, and most people just say okay. If you resist, you will usually get a verbal warning and a repeated request to comply. If you still resist, then we will make you comply. There is a small percentage of people that decide to resist the arrest at this point and put themselves in more legal trouble and increase the chance of bodily injury. Even if the arrest is still debatable, in the mind of the civilian at this point, the process is underway for them to be arrested. There is a legal proceeding that needs to take place. Civilians still have rights, legal counsel, and due process. If the arrest was unlawful, then they will have due process and the opportunity for a court to hear their side of the story. Fighting a cop that's trying to put you under arrest is never going to go well for you. They have lethal and non-lethal tools at their disposal, and if they feel fearful for their lives, they may use their tools to defend themselves or protect their partner.

When a call for service is initiated, it's all about the behavior. Suppose you're waving around a machete. We don't know what you're thinking. We don't know how you're feeling. You look angry. You might be frightened. You might be delusional or hallucinating; we are trying to sort that out. That is when the crisis intervention team training kicks in. The mental health advocates, the ones I work with, were making statements such as the police have to stop shooting people who are in a mental health crisis. I agree that would be great; however, if that person's doing something dangerous and about ready to seriously hurt or kill someone, I will use a taser or deadly force. Your mental state has nothing to do with where that machete is being swung. We don't want to use deadly force on anyone, but we have to stop the behavior that could harm us and everyone around us.

ASSESS THE BEHAVIOR

In some situations, the officer may conclude that an investigation is necessary to ensure lawful compliance is achieved. A good and well-trained officer will conduct his or her investigation and bring about a conclusion. They may issue them a warning or a ticket for an infraction. In a lawful encounter, the officer can do his due diligence and make sure the person has no outstanding warrants or anything that would prohibit the officer from releasing that person back into the public after their investigation is concluded. The officers are in a position to ensure that traffic tickets are paid, and past judgments are enforced to facilitate the due process judgments presented in the court of law.

At the end of the day, if you think about the purpose of an actual law, it is deduced down to behavior. If someone is speeding, they are acting unacceptably to the standards set for that street. The law setters have deemed that behavior to be unacceptable. The police officer is then able to investigate the suspected unacceptable behavior and seek compliance to prohibit the future breach of said behavior.

WHAT TYPE OF BEHAVIOR ARE YOU OMITTING?

Police work is not pretty; everything I just mentioned is not fun. The investigation is not fun; the confrontation is not fun; the enforcement of the law is not fun. It's not fun for an ordinary citizen, and it's definitely not fun for a criminal career. Until this point, we have concluded that law enforcement is necessary to protect people's rights and the state's interest in its society. We want someone to call to come in and help enforce civility and harmony. If someone's trying to rob the bank, we want someone to represent us and ensure our money is protected. If someone's causing a domestic disturbance or starting cars on fire, we want someone to be able to go in and stop those harmful behaviors.

There are major safety issues that happen every single day. If you have your hand in your coat pocket, and you're sticking your finger like a gun, a cop sees you and says, "Hey, take your hands out of your pocket." You reply, "I don't want to. Make me. You have no right to arrest me." If you are suspected of committing a crime or about to commit a crime, then the officer has the right to investigate. So, the cop pulls out their gun because they feel you may have one that you're concealing. When the cop pulls their gun out, the civilian starts screaming. Why do you have your gun out? Why are you being a jerk? I would ask, why aren't you doing what the officer says? How hard is it to pull your hands out of your pockets? These encounters can turn deadly in split seconds. If your emotional response to the officer is interpreted as threatening, you could be putting yourself in harm's way.

Suppose someone is arrested and on their way to court. They will generally get dressed in a suit or something nice and show up with their lawyer who advises them on their entire legal process and they appear before a judge wearing something very nice and acting well-mannered. If they act out in court, the judge will typically tolerate 3 seconds of bad behavior until they're held in contempt and jailed. Some judges will tape the person's mouth shut so they can proceed with the trial. In most cases, no judge will tolerate any behavior that doesn't fall under the umbrella of being well-mannered. It makes you wonder about the outcome if people behave well-mannered in front of the officer who is delivering lawful orders. How would those encounters turn out better if the civilian was well-mannered and diffused conflict alongside the officer? I wonder how many more police encounters can go without incident because both the officer and civilian are acting in a non-threatening manner.

People don't always like to go to jail for things that they do wrong. If you sit down next to a gangster on the street who's dealing drugs and ask him if he would like to go to jail? He will say hell no, I'm going to do everything I can to stay away from the popo. The gangster is going to put up a big fight. They will do everything they can do to prevent themselves from going to jail. If that means starting a police chase, an officer-involved shooting, or harming other people as they try to avoid being arrested. They're going to do everything in their power to ensure they don't go to jail again. Do they increase their chances of getting into a bad altercation with officers because they don't want to go to jail for their behavior? Of course, this happens every day. Criminals aren't on their best behavior in front of cops. They tend to put themselves in more trouble.

TAKING RESPONSIBILITY FOR YOUR BEHAVIOR

People's behaviors out in public are really getting out of control. No one should be able to riot, damage property, start police stations on fire, and cause others bodily harm for any cause. That behavior is destructive in every way. No good, noble cause should produce such harmful, destructive behaviors. We can't allow behaviors that harm ourselves, the public, and our property. It's unacceptable. When is it ever okay for the cops to allow someone to burn your business down to the ground or vandalize your home? When is it okay for them to set your car on fire or steal your identity? The laws are a helpful standard that provides us with guardrails to life, liberty, and the pursuit of happiness. They're there to protect us and to protect our things. If anything were to ever happen to us or our things, there's a system and a process in place that has our back, and due process will find its course. We can have advocates and a system to fight for us. That's the hope in our legal system. That's the hope in our laws. The assurance and protections are why we have police officers. They hold us accountable, and they also hold everyone else accountable.

The more accountability we accept personally, the better our lives will be. The amount of accountability we give ourselves will be extended to those we meet. We will be more accountable at work and when we encounter law enforcement. The measure of change that we desire to see in our lives and our community is directly tied to our level of personal responsibility. This means we need to stop blaming others for how we feel, think, and act. It is possible to behave in a manner that is civil, professional, and respectful to those that we encounter. We have the power to manage our emotions, thoughts, and actions. No one makes us do anything we don't want to do, we're not controlled by anyone but ourselves.

Here are a few ridiculous stories where people are quick to point the finger at someone else when they should be taking responsibility for their own actions. I had a neighbor one time that lived with her sister. They would use their mower to trim their hedges. They lift up a push lawn mower and trim the hedges. One day she lifted the mower up to trim her hedges and it trimmed off a few of her fingers. Now, on every lawn mower, you'll see a picture of a blade going through fingers because of a lawsuit. Do you think that's a manufacturer problem or a user error?

If you live in a house with a sidewalk out front, and someone slips and falls, whose fault is it? Is it your fault or the person who fell? Why can't people take responsibility for their own actions? It's a sad reality that everyone starts looking at who they can blame instead of realizing they fell on their own.

Whose fault is it if you pour hot coffee on yourself? Is it the person who made the coffee or the manufacturer of the coffee? Do you remember the famous lawsuit regarding McDonald's? If you buy a pizza oven and burn yourself with it, you should try to sue the manufacturer for your carelessness. Really? Did the pizza oven get hot? What should you do around hot things? Let's keep the legitimate claims on the path to due process and eliminate the reckless blame game we try to play on others.

GOOD COP, BAD COP

Are there cops that act out of line and push the limit too far? Absolutely. Cops get emotional and act out sometimes. Some cops have bad intent and behave unacceptably. Some cops are bad altogether and they should never be cops. They should be held accountable for their actions. We'll talk about some of the underlying problems that policing has today and cold hard facts that are evident. There is an understood and perceived authority that comes with policing. Officers should be sensitive and compassionate because of the power that they carry. They can wield compliance in the name of the law, which should be a protected and sacred duty. Not everybody does it right; when people are out of line, they should be taught the right way to do things. They should be held accountable when their actions are unlawful.

Every cop doesn't always live up to the best standards. Sometimes cops let us down. Maybe they made a mistake, thought we were someone else, or mistreated us. Sometimes there are cops that let their ego lead them instead of their lawful duties and their training. There are bad cops out there that desire evil things, and that is absolutely unacceptable. Sometimes the judicial system lets us down. However, those bad situations and bad cops are not the norm. Our system does work, and our police force is wholeheartedly there to do good. We can't let the news amplification of one case or another cloud our judgment to think that a large majority of police encounters end in undesirable outcomes. All we have to do is look at the statistics of police encounters to see the reality.

Cops should be held accountable, and so should people. Okay, hold on a second. Cops go to basic academy and receive on average 820 hours of training. Of course some states have more and some less, and this can vary within a state. They also receive field training, specialized unit training, and sensitivity training based on their department and their city/county/state agency. Some receive crisis intervention training along with a host of other mental health type training. Anytime an undesirable outcome occurs with the police officer, the public generally decides the cops should go to more training. What if any accountability, emotional regulation, or behavioral management training is provided to and required of civilians? Should neighborhoods learn how to act publicly and undergo emotional regulation training? What level of training is sufficient for officers or civilians in order to prevent needless loss of life? What if there are ten times more police calls for domestic disturbances on one block compared to the rest of the city? Should the city require the block to undergo some preventative training?

Cops can do better in some areas. Cops can use less force when encountering people with mental illness if they see the signs. Through training, some key indicators are visible that should tell the officer they are encountering someone with a mental illness. Education will help us use less force. This is just one example of ways cops can do a better job. I will always remember my family saying which started with my grandfather, who was born in 1898. "Buck up chap; you will get through this, don't quit. God helps those that help themselves. There is a place for your feelings, but don't let those feelings hold you back from becoming the best version of yourself in this moment."

CHAPTER 3

Society

IN SEARCHING FOR ANSWERS TO SOME OF THE PROBLEMATIC AREAS we see today, it's impossible to overlook the direct and indirect impacts of society on us. Society consists of the people and the institutions around us, our shared beliefs, and our cultural ideas. Society speaks to the largest areas in our life, like our family, religion, education, etc. I want to look at some changes over time within our society and how they affect us today. I will focus more on some areas of society and the future chapters because they surround so much of our life.

I am not a sociology expert; however, I've taken a considerable amount of time to study the human brain, and I've assisted people in behavior and the study of that behavior for decades of my life. Given my past in law enforcement, my perspective may be a new consideration for some of you. In the most recent days of my life, I sit across from people and talk about their observations and problems. Within those observations, it's hard not to paint a picture of how I saw myself 20, 30, and 40 years ago versus today. I know you did the same thing; you think about how things were in the past and come up with some form of conclusion about if they're better or worse. I believe it's a normal process; we all do it.

My considerations often go beyond myself into realms of society. Because I'm a part of the piece that helps maintain order within society as a former LEO and now counselor, I often think about the ramifications of how society impacts what I do. The officers that come and see me for counseling speak about the impacts of society on what they do. They tell me about interactions with certain cultures and religious groups. They speak to me about the differences between dealing with someone poor and someone rich. We converse about family dynamics and everything that surrounds family interaction.

After a while, it seems there's such a stark comparison in some specific areas that are very different than before. In some ways, we have new problems; in others, our problems have just been exacerbated. Are things better? Overall, there are many better things, but I can't help but try to improve the areas that need more attention. The parts that are eroding. I meet with people one-on-one to deal with these things, and this book and this chapter are an extension of that for me to try to do my part and help our society by sharing what I know.

FAMILY

If society were a car, that car's engine would be the family. The family unit is a small composite of what we see in society. If your family unit is thriving at home, you will be a productive member of society. If your family unit is broken when you believe that would spill over into society in many ways, perhaps in how you associate with those broken areas. For example, if you have a one parent home, studies show you are deprived of proper balance and care. Furthermore, if you are missing your father figure, you may be void of helpful fatherly interactions that deposit confidence, strength, accountability, and vision. If the parent you are missing is your mother, you may be void of helpful care, compassion, and nurturing interactions going into society.

I understand that our parents do their best, but we also realize that our upbringing does affect how we approach the world. If we received a less-than experience or an experience with a great deal of conflict and trauma, that would carry into everything we do. I would call it less than ideal. The realization is that the mindsets we formed as a child stick with us once we get older. If our parents were criminals, perhaps we would be exposed to things and situations that would be less than ideal. That puts us in a place where our brain is trained around those normalities. We even see the crimes they committed as options for us as we decide how we want to act and behave.

It's a very different reality if you were raised in a home where crime is common, versus the comfort of two loving parents. I don't want to shame anyone; I'm just pointing out the obvious underpinnings that feed our mindsets and behaviors. We still have ultimate control over ourselves, and just because we received a less-than-ideal upbringing doesn't mean we become bad people or do bad things. However, we must go through a process to retrain our brains around things that are helpful to ourselves and our families. I know many people that were raised in a single-parent home where the father was missing. It was difficult for them for some time, but through one avenue or another, books or mentors, they were able to get the help they needed to overcome their past troubles, and it motivated them to be the best parent possible.

On the other hand, during my years of law enforcement, I encountered people every day who did not get the help they needed to overcome their past traumas and troubles. Sure enough, they reproduced problems that their family participated in. They reintroduced domestic violence, drugs, guns, and crime because that was the life presented to them. I have compassion for them, while I also have to uphold the law. If they're committing crimes, they will have an issue with law enforcement and the court system.

They may actually hate the people enforcing the law because they behave like criminals. They may feel like cops aren't necessary because they only cause problems. They may have an internal bias that says every cop is bad because every time they've encountered a police officer, their situation didn't improve. They may teach their kids to be adversarial, combative, and difficult to any law enforcement officer they encounter. Why would they do this? They're choosing not to change and conform to the harmonious society we have constructed. They prefer to do their own thing, commiting crimes if they feel like it or out of the department store because they don't have enough or breaking into people's homes because they want what someone else has. The standard is not supposed to change because criminals no longer feel like behaving.

The only way society can continue in a semblance of order is for there to be a standard that we live by; unfortunately, that standard requires us to be accountable for our actions. Criminals need consequences. And the only people teaching you to be soft on crime are the criminals. Everyone else is perfectly happy with their harmonious society because they don't go around stealing stuff or hurting people. They are completely content with walking down the street and not fearing for their safety from a police officer because they've done nothing wrong. They appreciate the standard. They know they will be held accountable if they break the standard. That's enough motivation for them not to want to commit any crimes. So they work hard for their money and don't try to take it from someone else. If someone's trying to convince you that we don't need police officers anymore, what are they trying to get away with? What crimes are they trying to commit?

WE MODEL BASED ON WHAT WE SEE AT HOME

Children are far more intuitive than we give them credit for. They see our work through our emotions, plan and prepare, and work hard at the task at hand. They see us push through and persevere when we're not feeling good about the nuances of our decisions. They mirror the traits that we show them in how we handle ourselves and handle stressful situations. This mirroring is how they plan their own life. It's the model that they're shown. If a parent's natural reaction is to get furious and angry, then they're showing their child how to do that as well.

Can we expect kids to see a furious and angry parent and not act out in school? What if it's the only behavior they've seen modeled to express their frustration? They only have one option to go to when they're mad. It's easy to extend this framework into how children would grow up and behave in society based on the modeling that their parents gave them. Were the parents overprotective? Did they care more about the child's feelings than about doing what's right? Did they coddle the child? Today we're seeing more and more of this coddling and feelings of consideration over the understanding that they are the child and you are the parents.

Sure, consider your child's thoughts and feelings, but should you do so if it is an attempt to avoid parenting? When you tell a

3-year-old it's time to go to bed, is it time to go to bed? If so, then it's time to go to bed. Their feelings aren't really an issue with the directive that it's time to go to bed. I know it sucks telling your kids they have to do something they don't want to do. It's somewhat like a confrontation. They're going to push back and tell you that you're the worst person on the planet. They're going to make you feel terrible about making them go to bed. What should we do? Should we just let them make their own decisions and boss us around based on their feelings? That's what a lot of people do right now. It's framing our society in a way where we have teachers with 12 students in their classrooms, and when they run a competition, everyone gets the same trophy because they don't want anyone to feel bad about getting last. I just heard of a celebratory story from a High School Principal who was so proud that she could hide the honor roll students from being announced so her lesser-than-students in her school wouldn't feel bad. Is this what we want to do to help our kids achieve the best things in life? Hide their successes, so other kids don't feel bad?

I know it may sound like a silly example, but these kids become young adults, and then they become adults. Their mannerisms and behaviors are trained by their parents and their upbringing. They present themselves to society in the way they were taught. We would expect some of them to act out because they never learned to manage their emotions. They were never taught that there were consequences to their actions. They never learned different ways to cope with their frustration and overcome their struggles. In some ways, I expect these kids to present themselves in law enforcement situations in the future, because they didn't learn the life skills necessary to be productive members of society.

POLICING DIFFERENCES

Looking back at how things were and how things are now presented a lot of stark differences. It's easy to see some progressive changes that may not be so good. Back in the 80s, cops would always say, "I'm not a goddamn social worker. I'm a law enforcement officer." I'm not saying that's how it should be, but the common mentality back then was about enforcing the laws; we hold you accountable for your behaviors. Cops hold people accountable for their behavior, enforce the laws of the city, the county, and the state, and keep people safe. Besides eating donuts, they help with numerous things like medical assistance calls, domestic disturbance calls, criminal work like searching for suspects in a crime, and in a small percentage of these encounters, they sometimes have to use force. Like when there's an active shooter at a school, and yes, at times when assisting with mental health calls. They're trained to do crash analysis when someone gets into an accident to determine if the facts align with what people are saying. Those are just common things that cops do every single day. However, it has become more of a social worker role over the years. The new mentality is because of a certain situation, this law doesn't really matter; or that law doesn't really matter. Or, we don't have room in our jails, so we need to stop arresting people for certain crimes.

Let's discuss drugs, for example. Some people get caught with minor stuff like possessing marijuana where it's still unlawful. They may be a low-level user who is looking at self-medicating. Or, they may be the person who's in charge of distribution or creation for many others. The courts are more compassionate towards the self-medicating user versus the drug dealer, and we can see it in their sentence. But now, law enforcement and the courts are in the business of helping people with their personal treatment and self-medicating processes. In my opinion, that's not what cops are supposed to do. That's what social workers are supposed to do. That's not police work.

I'm not saying that someone shouldn't help them with their self-medicating use of different drugs. I think they should. I'm just not sure if it's law enforcement's job to do the work of a social worker because the jails are too full. If the jails are too full, don't we have a bigger societal problem that we need to address versus changing the job of the law enforcement officer? Doesn't that sound backward? What is the standard that we would like to accept in society? It's okay to commit crimes because there is no consequence. Eventually, if we continually lower our standard of, let's say, law enforcement, what does society become if there's no accountability? What does society look like when all those people that are arrested for criminal offenses are free to roam the streets acting in any manner that's fitting to them with pure lawlessness? Perhaps we will never see a day like that, but where does it stop? It's a slippery slope when we lower our standards.

WHICH LAWS CAN COPS ENFORCE?

Some laws are just being overlooked because of politics. No longer enforceable because the officers are asked to look the other way, or they're put in a position where it's nearly impossible for them to cite someone for certain offenses anymore. Here's an example of disorderly conduct from the 90s. I remember getting officially told by our people that the city's attorney's office would no longer prosecute people for disorderly conduct if no citizens around were disturbed. When the prosecuting office tells you they're not going to prosecute something, then what's the point of arresting someone for it? It will literally be a waste of your time and everyone else's time. The county attorney handles the prosecution. They can't tell the cops what to arrest for or what not to arrest for, but the county attorney will tell the sheriff and the municipalities and city agencies under them that we are not going to prosecute these cases. Don't bring them to us unless you have what we want to see.

Back in the day, people used to call out to police officers and say 'Popo'. Many of you are familiar with that phrase. The phrase may seem synonymous with a police officer, but it means that someone has spotted a law enforcement officer. The term came from low level encounters that were disrespectful. Whether the citizen was being disrespectful, or the officers were being disrespectful and the encounter usually went south, it turned into a criminal charge of 'Piss-Off-Police-Officer'. One end of the spectrum ended up adopting the term and it became used equally by both. So, imagine pulling up in your police car and someone's irate and yelling at you. It's 2:00 in the morning, and people are screaming and yelling at the top of their lungs, and you've got apartment buildings all around. They're creating such a disturbance that people are turning their lights on and trying to find out what's happening outside.

Now, as an officer, you'll tell them to quiet down, or they'll get in trouble. They go through the procedure, ask, tell, and make. The officers would say you're going to be arrested for disorderly conduct. That would be a common occurrence back in the day. But the prosecutor said they wouldn't prosecute anybody for disorderly conduct anymore if there weren't witness testimonies to the disorderly conduct.

So even though the person was committing disorderly conduct, the officers on the scene needed to find a collaborating witness testimony to arrest them. It didn't matter if that the person was affecting 10,000 people sleeping in an apartment building next door. They were not arrestable if they were by themselves without a third-party witness other than the officers.

So, we were stuck. Here we got a guy at 2 in the morning causing a scene. If we leave him, he may end up yelling and waking up the entire neighborhood. Who knows? Now I have to walk up to a stranger and see if they will collaborate with what's going on so I can take their name down, and then I can arrest the guy. When prosecutors and defense attorneys start setting the standard for criminal action, in essence the tail starts wagging the dog.

Prosecutors are also changing their stance on how much marijuana you need to carry for there to be a felony charge. In the late 80s, the felony amount of marijuana was 44 Grams, which was basically 2/3 of a sandwich bag. There were so many people that were arrested during that decade with marijuana, that the prosecutors changed their stance on who they would actually charge. The county attorney told everyone they would only charge people for 40 lb of marijuana instead of 44 grams. So, from that day forward, if you arrested someone for carrying an illegal amount of marijuana it was 39 pounds worth, they wouldn't receive a felony charge. Did the county attorney change their stance because the jails were filled to the brim with people selling weed? Was the problem so big that they had to change their approach to be more lenient with the problem? I guess, in some ways, the desired outcome of the County Attorney has transpired in some states, making marijuana legal for personal and recreational use. Is that because society gave in on the idea of it being a problem, or is it because they couldn't control the problem? Hence, the next best decision was to make it legal. Is it the same thing that happened with prohibition? One day, alcohol is against the law; the next, it's not. Which has nothing to do with whether or not it's good for you or whether any real studies say marijuana is okay to consume. It's just too new of a drug that comes to research. It seems like there are some benefits to cerebral traumas and diseases. Marijuana seems to do a really good job of blocking out certain things in your brain.

I heard of an officer getting in trouble for their language when no one could hear him. The cop was in their squad car driving to an emergency call. And, of course, some people do some interesting things when you're driving with lights and sirens. Someone pulled out in front of him on his way to a 911 call, and he said oh f*** as he swerved away from an accident. The word harmed no one. No one heard it, but technically, the public can if they make a records request with the city. The cop got into trouble for speaking to himself in his car. Was the cop being human or unprofessional by his reaction? Do you think he should be punished for speaking to himself when he was avoiding an accident?

HANDLE YOUR OWN CRIMINALS

A new trespassing trend has started to pop up in democratically led cities where trespassing becomes the responsibility of the property owner. The cops can issue a trespassing citation, but they wouldn't be allowed to remove the person from the property. They would say they've trespassed, but you are the owner and must physically remove them from the property. Hopefully, you don't get into a physical altercation with the trespassed individual. Try not to get into an assault when removing them from your property, but it's your responsibility to take care of this.

We seem to be in the middle of a pressure cooker situation with these things. Do you seriously expect an elderly individual to physically remove someone from their property who's trespassing and who's received a trespassing citation? Were the rights to an individual's property and space considered when they made this change? How about if the individuals in your house need to be trespassed? Are you going to physically remove them from their property without getting into a physical altercation with someone who's not supposed to be there? Seems pretty ridiculous to me.

Many agencies have a no-chase policy now and the criminals know this. Suppose I witness an infraction, or spot potentially criminal activity. I can't get in my car and chase them if they start fleeing. So this police car with the lights behind you no longer means anything. They laugh and drive away. They drive away at high speed and know the cop can't chase them.

So why not try to leave because you don't have consequences for that, and it's easier to escape and get away. You know, whether it's a low-level crime, and they don't go to jail, they don't do this, or the high-level stuff, the consequences for the criminals just keep getting lighter and lighter and lighter. That's part of the criminal culture, and they know that the cops are being handcuffed increasingly more, and it's getting easier for them to do their stuff. And all across the nation, again, you're seeing rising crime rates.

Why is crime going up? I've heard mayors and others who are liberal and supporting this, saying what are you doing about the crime? They don't want the cops to really enforce anything; they want to wave a magic wand so that we can prevent crime. The magic term for this magical act is called crime prevention. Crime prevention is the public's responsibility to hide anything that may look visible to someone who could take it. It's telling people they should lock their doors. Essentially it's an extension of a neighborhood watch. Is crime prevention enough to stop criminals from being criminals?

There's a story of a cop riding on a train in one of the local departments here. He came across this guy and asked, "Hey, do you have your fare ticket?" And the guy didn't, so he started dealing with them. And he says, "Hey, are you here illegally?" He was a Hispanic guy. The officer says, "Do you have your papers? Are you here legally?" And some person sitting on the train says, "Are you allowed to ask that question?" It's a touchy subject, right?

This was a while back, but it was still part of the immigration issues and the sanctuary cities, so it's politically charged. The cop looked at him and said, probably not. Well, there was a guy who was filming with his phone. And then the guy says, you should leave him alone. Well, that video got turned over to a news station. It was on the nightly news and became a big deal. The cop was put on administrative leave. They were going to fire him because of the question that he asked, but they offered him earlier retirement. Do you think the cop should enforce the law about someone being in the country illegally? Let's be clear here... cops are sworn to uphold all local, state, and federal laws! It's the politics that start to limit them. I can tell you a million stories about how society has imposed new rules on policing in the past few years. Most of these stories aren't so good. In my opinion, good is a measurement of harmony in society. The number of crimes committed in a city. The number of violent crimes that are committed in a city. The number of drug overdoses, suicides, and depression. Are all measurements to determine what level of "good" is. I guess if you ignore these numbers, then the erosion is okay.

There's this thing called the bell curve. Starts off low on the left-hand side and then mounds up in the middle, and then it swoops back down to be the same level on the other side. The majority of everyone's in the middle, and the people acting out the most extreme are on the right or the left. This is visible in politics with the democrats and the republicans. The most extreme points of view go the furthest away from the center. The same happens in society. Those who act out the most and scream the loudest always get attention. If you are a logical, rational thinker and you would like to debate something or have a discussion, you're probably not going to draw a big crowd because you're not acting in a way that seems extraordinary.

If you wanted to get a big crowd around, you would need to do something to draw attention to yourself. You may need to light cars on fire. Vandalize a few buildings. Say some racial things. That would give you the attention that you're seeking. Our society is designed around attention-seeking people. Every day they chase their likes and followers online on their social accounts, and if you give them more attention for acting out, guess what they're going to do? Act out. We should consider this the next time someone acts out before us. Should we reward this behavior by posting about it, talking about it, and sharing it online? Or should we celebrate and promote healthy behavior, especially the kind that builds a successful, productive society? It seems like we have a lot of people chasing the bad actors around town instead of modeling the way things should be. Society is nothing more than individuals put together. If we can individually become something great, then our society will become different.

CHAPTER 4

Politics

POLITICS IS EVERYONE'S FAVORITE WORD. The practice of politics is associated with the governance of a country or specific area. However, we see most people in politics are just looking to promote themselves to obtain power or money. Over the years, we've seen politics morph and change tremendously. The wielding of one's vote permits a person or a group so much influence and power that they'll do anything to garnish attention from those individuals and keep them interested in the governing activities. Unfortunately for all of us, that means we will be provided messaging and content that is unnerving and emotionally charging to provoke us into action.

Meaningful events take place every day. Whether they're good or bad, an underlying agenda either accelerates a political party or takes away from their momentum. The party doesn't remain in power by picking the middle of the road and avoiding controversial topics. No, parties remain in power because of controversy. They need to be able to communicate to their audience the most extreme cases of conflict. This doesn't mean that the conflict needs to be true. Often we're given bite-sized pieces of a situation in order for a narrative to be formed that is clean and easily deliverable.

Take George Floyd, for example. Cops are called out for a routine 911 call of someone using counterfeit money. At the end of the call, someone had tragically died.. George Floyd's death gripped the United States. It sparked a movement within the Democratic party and Black Lives Matter; riots, looting, and all types of crime shot up in the days subsequent to his death. Communities were gripped with the reality that they were no longer safe because of nightly protests, vandalism, and burglaries. I don't typically examine police cases that go on today because I've seen enough. Generally, I like to disconnect from it because I spent several decades immersed in it. However, I'd like to speak to components within the George Floyd case.

The police officer that kneeled on George Floyd's neck and back should never have done that. Perhaps he might have done that for a very quick second, but not to the extent that he did. That was absolutely wrong. A reasonable police officer would not have done that for that amount of time. Law Enforcement Officers do make mistakes. It appeared to me that that was a blatant mistake. Some mistakes are criminally prosecutable, especially when they're tied to someone being hurt or a loss of life. I don't believe that the officer intended to murder someone that day. He did, however, make several mistakes that could have definitely affected the life of George Floyd.

If we take a step back and look at the situation surrounding that police call, we see the police are called to the scene because someone was using counterfeit currency. They arrest George Floyd and find out he had prior convictions. George Floyd likely knew that if he were arrested for this, it probably wasn't going to be good.

He may potentially go back to jail for quite some time. Also, the police found white pills in the car, which they would have been able to test for drugs. The cops may or may not have known he ingested a lethal dose of fentanyl. According to an expert pathologist, when George Floyd consumed the fentanyl, he had about 8 to 9 minutes to live, based on the amount in his system. This was because of the amount he consumed, coupled with his underlying heart problems. According to the pathologist, he would have died in the car if they weren't touching him.

Suppose we push all the facts and speculation aside. What is the appropriate response based on what the officer did and based on what George Floyd was doing? Well, George Floyd was committing a crime and died in police custody. The officers on the scene should have handled things differently. Did they set out to kill someone that day? I don't think so. However, someone did die, and this became the center of a political uproar about police brutality and racism. Regardless of the facts, the police were perceived as evil, and George Floyd was made a saint. He was a martyr for other African American communities. Some feel like the police are blatantly targeting them.

As I pointed out in the previous chapters, police work is not pretty; in this case, there were some very disturbing images. The cop was clearly doing some things wrong, and George Floyd was clearly committing a crime while on drugs. It was a mess of a situation. For any normal person, that would be alarming to see. Watching someone die on a video is never pleasant and will stir up the deepest emotions in people that don't typically see that. For a lot of people, this became emotionally enraging. Their internal biases may be confirmed in the images and videos that they saw. People felt enraged and threatened by the actions of George Floyd and these police officers. This started a violent movement that fueled the political debates to defund police departments around the country.

Police encounters are very common. Every year in the United States, there are upwards of 60 million police encounters. They range from someone getting a speeding ticket all the way to police chases and arresting murderers. Studies show that less than 1% of police encounters include a threat of force where a police officer needs to verbally or physically show a threat of force in order for them to get the suspect to complyor end in the use of force. If the suspect is told to comply and instead chooses to start fighting the police officer, then force may be used. So the police encounters in the entire year, a threat of force or use of force constitutes for less than 1% of all police encounters. Which percent do you feel will be used for political purposes in the media, online, and up for debate? Of course, it's the 1%.

I'd like to lay some perspective for you so we understand how politics can affect the way we see policing and our communities. I will be the first one to tell you that cops are human, just like everybody else, and they make mistakes. I will also admit that some bad cops do bad things. They need to be held accountable for their behavior because of their tremendous responsibility. However, 99% of all police encounters are not exciting enough for the media to cover them. They don't contain the viral or trend worthy components to politicize them. The police officers didn't get caught doing something illegal or bad, the citizens complied with the officer's request, and everybody went on their merry way.

The 1% of time when force is used, only 1% of those times is the force considered unreasonable. So, only the .001% use of force makes for good TV. It's something that is emotionally stirring. As a politician, that's what you want to use to talk about; how mean and violent the cops are against innocent people. The cops encounter this person because of a 911 call or suspicious behavior. The threat of force or use of force is most likely because of the suspect deciding not to cooperate. Suppose cops go to arrest someone suspected of a homicide. In most cases, it's up to the suspect to decide if they are going to escalate the encounter into a threat of force or use of force.

In 2014 the famous Michael Brown incident took place in Ferguson, Missouri. "Hands up, don't shoot", was the catchy phrase quoted by one person at the scene who fabricated some details in order to create a narrative.. They said that Michael Brown was shot "execution style" by a racist and angry officer. The facts came out about the case; Michael Brown, in fact, fought the police officer, and his DNA was found on the officer's gun. The officer shot Michael Brown in the ensuing fight, perhaps fighting for his life. Facts sometimes take a while to come out because of proper due process with the court systems. trend worthy moments and catchy phrases don't care about the facts. The Michael Brown incident was a symbol of the lack of trust between the African-American communities and law enforcement. The idea of police officers singling out African Americans to kill them was echoed across America in the world. This incited violent protests that caused billions of dollars of damage and needless, harmful encounters against police officers and others.

How could this be? How could the media convey things so far away from the facts? That's what the media and politics do. It doesn't need to be factual for it to provoke an emotional response from someone. If there's a narrative that police officers are bad and money and power can be gained by conveying this, then every little sliver of perspective will go in that direction. Well, how can someone gain money and power by saying police officers are bad? The answer is easy, when you're rallying a group of people and collecting votes, votes equal power. When someone is in office, they decide where the money goes. First to themselves and then to things that keep them in power.

Unfortunately and fortunately, that is how our system is set up. Political parties participate in narratives that feed division amongst themselves. They must portray the other party as evil, hypocritical, uncompassionate, and, most of all, wrong. A common person needs to see the stark contrast between their political party versus the other. This accentuates the bell curve that we see in society. Those representing our political parties are not typically in the middle. They are on the furthest extremes on either side.

WHAT'S THE AGENDA TODAY?

If you look at politics today, it is very different from how it was a few decades ago. The arguments change as party lines change. If a politician feels like their narrative doesn't fit their political party, then they simply change it. Today, we have a very wishy-washy political environment. It's very easy to see liars and hypocrites every day in politics. They say one thing because it's what their party wants them to say, and then they do the opposite. Sometimes these agendas are party lines that they're told to abide by. However, history brings us evidence of both parties being on the wrong side.

The Democratic Party champions itself as being the party of minority groups and marginalized people. However, in the past, the Democratic Party was strongly opposed to ending slavery. They fought the Republicans hard all the way through the Civil War to keep slavery in place. They strongly opposed the concepts of Human Rights, especially the rights of Native Americans. They pushed forth bills and efforts for ethnic cleansing, genocide, and other horrendous things against the Native Americans. They opposed several laws that included public schools where everyone could be integrated. They didn't want the mixing of whites and blacks in public schools.

The Republican Party, too, found itself on the wrong side of history. They pushed forth deliberate policies of USA imperialism. First seen in the Kingdom of Hawaii and the Spanish Colonial possession of the Philippines. The Republicans pushed to overthrow the queen of Hawaii and suppress the native culture. This was classic imperialism, as seen in European powers of the past.

This should open up our eyes to see that party lines emphasize power and money. The lines of argument change continuously through time. This should give us some perspective on politics and how it influences us. We want to be on the right side of history rather than giving our allegiance to one party or another.

EXTREMISM

It's not newsworthy unless it's extreme. That's why politics needs to be extreme. There's a thing that gets exploited with us about politics. It's called the negativity bias. If something is extreme and negative, we need to pay attention to it more than something that's good because it could potentially impact or harm us. If we see extreme images and pictures or hear exaggerated extreme words, we're more likely to pay attention. I believe this is occurring more because, again, people aren't held accountable for what they say/ do. One good example is Mayorkas. The politics of the border is so polar that people tied to the issue can say pretty much anything they want and there are no consequences. Another is Jean Pierre. In the middle of a US economic downturn with prices at the gas pumps and grocery stores at their highest, when asked about the economy, her response is, "We feel as though the economy is in a good place to turn around". Talk about blowing smoke up our back end! These provoking images and words will get a response from us because of our negativity bias. We need to know what the threat is to avoid it or fight against it. Anyone in politics can leverage this negativity bias to gain support for their ensued power.

We should be aware of this extremism to see it for what it is. If we're mindfully aware of the ridiculous bias that is presented to us, then we can disengage from its effect on us. We can appeal to a more rational sense of self. The side of us that uses rational thought, logic, patience, and facts to depict our world and how we should engage it. If we lose our sense of rational self, we'll be like the wind blowing from one extreme to another.

Let's unpack a few extreme ideas. One of the first ones that comes to mind is systemic racism in policing. I'll be the first person in line to stand up and say, if the cop is doing something criminal, make them pay. If they're doing something wrong, hold them accountable. That goes for any profession. There is no evidence of systemic racism in policing. I guarantee that there's no system that exists in Minneapolis or any of the agencies. I'm sure the rest of the country and the law enforcement agencies would agree with me that systemic racism does not exist, period. Is that something that may be built around the idea of an ultimate, negative negativity bias?

With our negativity biases, we hyper-focus on the negative situations and make them all-encompassing. Our human condition emphasizes our negative biases and convinces us of systematic and widespread problems. Depending on how much work is exposed to this negativity by us, it turns into a mindset and belief system. If you're alone and see a bear in the woods from a distance, you'll know they exist. The next night you're alone, and you hear a twig break behind you; your brain will go to the worst-case scenario every time. You're going to think that bears are about ready to kill you. That ingrained bias is to help you survive, but it can instill continual fear and irrational fears as well.

In the past several years, irrational fears have been propagated and promoted in politics. There wouldn't be as many political movements if true facts were held in context. People may not vote differently. Donations to nonprofits and to political parties might not happen. The only way for Maximum Impact is for there to be a perceived systematic problem. Out of this idea is where black lives matter emerged. When a black male gets shot, especially by a white cop, there's outrage. Regardless of the facts, this is a matter of protest. We don't care what the black male was doing. The narrative can spin off in a million directions. The classic example of this is from Spider-Man and the Daily Bugle. J. Jonah Jameson: "With Spider-Man nearby, trouble can't be far away. And you know what trouble means; Headlines! National coverage! So don't screw this up! I mean, uh, good luck."

With extreme perspectives or feelings just taking off, we don't check in with ourselves on the facts. We don't want to wait for all the evidence to come out in court and hear from all parties before we make our conclusion. Our feelings vindicate our biases, and therefore they run rampant. When we get to a heightened emotional state where we feel like our lives are in danger because of our fears, we're willing to do extraordinary things to display our anger and frustration. We may start protests and set cop cars on fire and declare people groups as evil. We may take one example, a police-involved shooting, and use it to justify every one of our negativity biases.

This bias becomes a belief system. Belief systems are not always subject to tangible or factual things. I could have a belief system that says all ice cream sellers are murders. Maybe my belief system is irrational, and it has no basis in fact, or maybe one time I saw an ice cream seller as a murderer in real life. I could live my life thinking that all ice cream sellers are murderers, and I avoid them at all costs because I found other people that agree with my belief system. I could start a movement that says there's a systematic problem with ice cream sellers. They all have this murderous trait they grow up with, and we need to do something about them. I must stop them from selling ice cream in our cities and try to remove all their funding.

Personally, I've never met a cop that pursues people based on the color of their skin and not based on their actions. I'm not saying they don't exist; I'm just saying I haven't met any. The question all the police officers that I know would ask, is the person doing something suspicious that would make them a suspect in an investigation. If so, then the police interaction would continue. We don't arrest people because of their skin color. So for all those that say there's systematic racism and policing, it's just not there. A systematic problem that police do have is that they are constantly looking for and dealing with criminals. Systematically, it's proven that if you are a criminal, you will more than likely have an encounter with police.

Cops don't care what your skin color is. They just care what you're doing. Cops are there to enforce the law, and they have to deal with the behavior. It may not seem right, and it may not feel right, but if your behavior warrants a police response, they will deal with it. We must always keep this in mind. Politics will never exacerbate the normal common scenarios. The only newsworthy thing is the extreme examples. This is done to "normalize" extreme bias. Perhaps a political party presents an idea about systematic racism continuously every single day in order to train us to think that there's actually systematic racism. Well, for seeing it every day, it must be everywhere, you would think to yourself. Don't forget that 99% of police encounters don't include a threat of force or use of force. It's clear to see there's not a systematic problem.

THE CONTINUATION OF POLITICAL POWER.

The way to start political power is to convince people of a narrative that gets them to act for you. When people run for office they run on ideas. Those ideas need to be provoking enough for people to follow them and provide them with money and power. They receive power as an effect of the influence they're gaining. However, money is the conduit and the reason. If you look at any political movement, it is encompassed around money. I would include black lives matter as a political movement. Currently, the organization hasn't funded anybody to go to school, and it hasn't paid for charitable meals for underprivileged kids. It has, however, spent money to get criminals out of jail and accumulated a lot of real estate in very expensive areas.

If you think about it for a second, where do your ideas get taught the most? In our school system, of course. This is why you see a continuation of the changing and indoctrination of ideas within our K-12 schools through graduate school. If a political party wants to change the narrative for the country, they need to start in the school systems by eliminating certain words from their vocabulary.

They would say certain words are offensive, even though they may be true. They would loosen the structure of something to create doubt. This has been evident throughout the years of the LGBTQ+ community. One day the word gay means happy, the next day, it means homosexual. One day, genders have been male and female since the beginning of time, and now we have 107 genders according to secualdiversity.org. One day, abortion is a medical professional decision; the next day, your political party decides for you. One day, cops are there to protect and serve; the next, they are evil, terrible monsters actively seeking to kill us.

Let's evaluate a reasonable approach to an extremely controversial subject, abortion. This has been highly politicized through the years; certain political parties are for it, and certain political parties are against it. When should a political party decide what to do with your body? Mind you, the people that are elected to office aren't necessarily qualified to speak to the inner parts of your body. Someone has unprotected sex and thinks they might have messed up. They decide to take a Plan B pill to shed the uterine lining, so the fertilized egg(s) don't attach. Respectfully, it's the same thing that we do with chickens. We don't let the eggs develop and remove them from the environment that allows them to form fully.

Now, did they wait too long and have a functioning baby inside of them with a brain, heart, and tiny toes? What would certain medical professionals say about the health of your pregnancy? Do you have a fully formed baby that can live independently after being pregnant for nine months? Should you tell your politician what to do about that 9-month-old baby? Isn't that a medical question, much like all your other internal medicine questions? Some people went to graduate school for over a decade to learn about this exact thing. Right now, it's popular to tell people what to do with their bodies, and we have allowed this conversation to become political rather than a personal medical decision. It will stay a political one because it's highly emotional.

Don't get drawn into the dark swamp on the far left or the far right. Hold fast to what you know to be true, and keep an open mind about what you're unaware of. I would encourage you to evaluate your information source to ensure that it's not just feeding you absolute and extreme perspectives. From time to time, you may want to moderate your media consumption to allow your brain to balance what's good and true about your life versus what is wrong about the world. Avoid creating new biases handed to you by a political party. If you're truly curious and understanding the situation, facts, and history, take time and learn from everyone about it. I always like to ask myself what this person has to gain by telling me this. If the result is money and power, they have every reason to manipulate me into following them. I like to think for myself, and therefore, I'm going to evaluate all the facts.

CHAPTER 5

Technology

WHETHER YOU LIKE IT OR NOT, we are in a technology curve that may never end. Unlike any time in history, the rapid advancement of our technology is hard to keep up with. I'm part of an older generation; some of my stories come from the 60s and 70s. I wouldn't naturally say that I'm tech savvy in any way, I'm pretty content with the simplicity of things. I am happy to embrace the technology curve in some ways. When the taser came out in the 90s, I was happy to adopt it and teach others how to use it. I was presenting information on the taser to one of our city civilian review committees once, and I asked for a volunteer to get shot with the taser, and nobody wanted to volunteer. So, I was happy to invite my wife and demonstrate the use of the taser in front of everyone. She went down like a sack of potatoes. I hope they were impressed with my comfortability using this on my spouse. But it's likely they just believed I didn't like her.

Our consideration of the use of technology and how it's implemented into our lives is a conversation that we should continue to have. We want to look at the benefits of what it's bringing us and how it's helping our lives somehow, like having a smart thermostat that regulates the temperature when you're not home or energy-saving appliances that do more with less energy. There is a true benefit to the acceleration of technology that is absolute. I remember when police cruisers didn't have computers, so if you needed to get certain police work done on the traffic stop, you had to take somebody to the station. Now, there's not only a computer in every cop car; we have a computer in our pocket smarter than the computers built ten years ago. Good technology allows us to do things more efficiently, faster and better in various ways.

ADVANCE US

For policing, hundreds, if not thousands, of new software advancements occur yearly. Physical technology like tasers, body cameras, and self-guided license plate scanners are just the tip of the iceberg regarding new technology that advances policing. In the last several years, facial recognition software has made finding criminals much easier. The US and several countries are now incorporating retinal scans to ID you before you get through customs. It's just another unique identification that allows the bad guys to get caught.

On a personal level, personal security has increased dramatically with technology. Now we have smart locks on our homes that can lock themselves if we leave them unlocked. Our cars can remind us that they're unlocked. Cars themselves can turn off if they've been stolen, and they're incorporating new technology where if you don't pay your monthly car payment on time, it can return itself to an impound lot. It's a fantastic time to be alive, and it's crazy to even think about some of the stuff that's being created.

Every day we benefit from advanced technology in one way or another. We usually don't know the back-end processes it takes to get our Amazon packages or get our oranges nice and clean, but we appreciate it. Technology is here to stay, and as we advance and become a modern technological society, we will see some tremendous things. These advancements bring us greater opportunities and expose us to new areas we need to become more familiar with. This leads us to some new problems we must be aware of. How can technology hurt us?

TENSION

I'm keenly aware that every interaction in policing could go to court. We take that understanding and couple it with the criminal nature of policing. A large percentage of the interactions make a no-mistake environment. If a police officer were to make a mistake, many people, including themselves, could die or go to prison. How many other professions are like that? If you make a mistake on the job, you could die or go to jail.

Locally, we had an incident where an officer pulled out a gun, thinking they were pulling out their taser to stop someone from fleeing. Do you remember the Dante Wright police shooting that made the national news? Let me fill in a bit of the back story so you understand some details the police officers would have known when they pulled him over.

Dante Wright can be seen online playing with a handgun that he used in an aggravated robbery sometime shortly before. Little did he know that he would be using social media to shed light on his mental state before he was ready to commit a crime. Investigators say he entered the victim's clothing to take their money at gunpoint. Wright was arrested five days later for this incident. He then violated the terms of his release by brandishing a firearm in public. This led to an outstanding warrant that he had. He was pulled over for a minor traffic infraction, and the police likely ran his plates while pulling him over. Wright was wanted on an active firearms warrant, had pending armed robbery charges, and had allegedly been involved in two other shootings in which one of the victims just died because of a gunshot wound to the head.

Body cam footage shows that they asked him to exit the vehicle. They went to arrest him. He fought the police officers and jumped back in his vehicle to flee. As he was driving away, the officers were wrestling with him. One of the officers, Kim Potter, intended to shoot him with her taser as he was about ready to drive away while they were still wrestling with him. Instead of using her taser, she mistakenly used her firearm and shot him, and he died.

Because of technology, we can watch the dashcams and body cams of police officers. We were able to replay the entire incident in real-time. The world was able to see from multiple angles precisely what took place. The court was able to see everything that was recorded, including audio and video. Kim Potter fell to the ground crying, knowing that she used her firearm instead of the taser, saying she would go to jail because of her mistake. The courts and the general public later agreed about the misuse of her firearm. Unfortunately, the suspect fought the police officers and lost his life in the encounter. Routine traffic stops don't end in people losing their life.

If Dante had correctly behaved, he would have been arrested and taken to jail for quite some time for his outstanding warrants. I imagine Dante didn't want to go to jail for a while, so he played his odds and tried to flee from the police.

THE CREATION OF THE DISTORTED, FAKE, AND CENSORED

Dante's fleeing from arrest because of his outstanding warrants somehow conveyed through various social media and media outlets as a racial shooting. Some compared him to Martin Luther King as a martyr for the African American community. How could this be with the facts of the case clearly visible to the public? Welcome to the dark side of the advancement of technology. Technology only accelerates our narratives and biases. If we intend to distort facts, spin narratives, and create drama, we will utilize the latest and greatest to do just that.

Not only did we receive real-time updates on the racist shooting of Dante Wright by Kim Potter on our smartphones to provoke some emotional response to us, but we were also shown partial, distorted, fake narratives that were paraded around at us as truth through social media continuously. Everyone took their liberties to create whatever story they felt fit their internal worldview. Corporate America, for sure, informed us that this racially involved shooting justified riots and protests. It was evident that cops were bad, and Dante was right. It was just another white cop shooting an unarmed black man.

If only the facts were conveyed as intended, instead, they had to fight being censored, and their posts were taken down online. Some had their post garnish significantly less traffic than they would typically because of the controversial nature of the subject matter. Or because anybody with a more conservative, realistic approach toward the facts was considered an uncompassionate racist.

In this case and probably every future case, people took liberties to create new news using the latest technology. They would generate AI images that have distorted truths to make it look like the police did things that they didn't do. It is incredible to see how you can put in a few words, and AI will generate an image exactly like what you commanded. News media outlets created every kind of disturbing image surrounding this so we could be fed whatever narrative they had in mind. YouTube and Google have internal systems on thumbnails and videos that reward certain facial expressions, emotional responses, and click-through rates. Because of these metrics, content is created to be more clickable, to provoke more of a response, and to feed a certain energy or fear.

When I'm at home, I turn on my Netflix occasionally and watch something. My interest is preloaded, and Netflix does a pretty good job recommending the shows I might watch. When I go to my sister's house to watch her dogs, her recommendations come up on Netflix. It's evident to me that all the action movies recommended to her are 80% women based. They know that she likes to watch action movies with primary female roles. Pretty cool.

On the other hand, if you have bad intentions in your heart or mind, you might surround yourself with watching things that feed that bad intent. If you're thinking about hurting someone and watching horror movies that end in terrible murders, then Netflix could be feeding you content that feeds your bad intent. It will recommend what you will likely watch, even though you may be watching things that lead you to do terrible things.

The same goes for searching things online and retargeting. I love the famous story from Target. A dad saw that his daughter was getting coupons and mail from Target surrounding pregnancy and motherhood. The dad went into Target and demanded to speak to a manager. He was irate that they would send his teen daughter ads and coupons for motherhood. The manager explained that every customer has an ID when purchasing a card or using their driver's license. Every purchase is tracked in the system so they can predict what they might be buying next.

The Target manager began to explain that when 25 very specific items are purchased together, there is an extreme likelihood that the purchaser is pregnant. Based on the facts, Target sent her ads for things related to someone who's about ready to have a child. The father went home and then found out his teen daughter was, in fact, pregnant, and Target knew about it before he did. That's crazy awesome and scary at the same time.

Our online search follows the same engagement-based funnel and retargeting. If we search things online using any of today's popular search engines, odds are we will be fed more and more of that content and ads to spark our continued interest. In social media, specific algorithms are actually geared around consumption-based content. Suppose you watch one police brutality video on YouTube, TikTok, or Instagram. You're going to see more police brutality videos. You'll be fed so many you won't know what to do with them. You might start to watch them continuously, thinking that's the only interaction that ever takes place in policing. You might start to form a bias around the continual consumption of this content. This is all because an algorithm feeds you the thing you may be interested in. This not only creates a more profound bias in us, but it also reinforces the extreme. We can binge-watch our negativity biases repeatedly to reinforce our bad ideas and behaviors.

Think about it for a second, without social media and lightning-fast news, how fast would our biases be formed in life? Would we have so many, and would they be so pronounced? Because of the current infrastructure with social media and technology, we could form a new bias over the weekend and be protesting it by Wednesday. That was unheard of when I was growing up.

I remember when the 1991 Rodney King riots happened

in Los Angeles. George Holliday recorded 12 minutes of footage of Rodney King's police encounter. Eighty-nine seconds of that footage went viral. George sold his video to the local news and then to the national news stations. Part of his footage was used to spark riots and protests in LA. Let me backup and fill you in on some of the details that took place. Robbery parolee Rodney King was on an eight mile chase through the streets of LA. He was going to be pulled over for speeding but refused.

After the eight mile chase, King and his occupants were told to exit the vehicle. King was intoxicated and decided not to comply even though his friends did. Four officers that responded to the call tried to force King down to arrest him, and he refused to comply with the arrest and fought them. The officers deploy their tasers on him twice to get him to submit to their arrest. This is where the footage kicks in from George Holliday. The video George recorded shows King rising to his feet after getting hit with the taser and charging toward one of the officers.

The video was inconsistent at parts but showed the officers fighting with King and striking him with a baton. The audio could not capture the police interaction because of the overhead helicopters. The police downplayed how many times they hit King, and the media downplayed the kind of person Rodney King was and what he was doing. In the end, the officers were acquitted on all charges. It provoked an uproar in the racially driven communities because all the officers were white.

The acquittals sparked the LA riots, which brought arson, looting, murder, and assaults to become the most destructive disturbance in the 20th century. This brought about three days of intense violence where 60 people were killed, more than 2,000 people were injured, and caused a billion dollars of property damage. On May 1st, President George W. Bush ordered military troops and anti-riot trained Federal officers to Los Angeles to stop the unrest.

A few of the officers were later charged with violating Rodney King's constitutional rights and with unreasonable use of force under the color of law.

LIGHTNING FAST NEWS

Finding fast news creates a warped perspective. As soon as all the fighting is done and the arrests are made, the suspect presents themselves before the court of the law sitting next to their lawyer. Looking in from the outside, we see lovely pictures of the dressed-up suspects wearing suits and ties, smiling with their families. When we see them in court they are dressed up like Sunday church with the best behavior on their face. It's time to dress up and look pretty. Make sure you're clean-shaven and have a fresh haircut for the judge and the public. You will do everything you can to persuade the jurors and the public to see it how you want them too.

Of course, we're only seeing these suspects/criminals on their best behavior. But that's not where we start to judge. We form our opinions before we see anything, let alone an 89-second clip of the end of a police encounter. Every single person is walking around with a cell phone that has the capability of live streaming or at least capturing images or recordings. Nowadays, everybody has an app on their phone where you can edit, change, and create based on the original recordings. In the courtroom, they can validate, properly sort and submit evidence. Some things don't make it to trial because it didn't get captured properly, such as they didn't have a warrant, and the evidence was manufactured or altered somehow. When it comes to the court of public opinion, anything that's trend worthy gets promoted. It doesn't have to be accurate; it doesn't have to be confirmed. As soon as something like a police shooting happens, preloaded PR reports will go out from specific organizations about racism and police brutality regardless of the facts.

I always get a kick out of the synced-up news stations. Anytime they want you to know something, they will repeat this exact phrase for about a week based on some talking points they were given. You can find it if you follow a vein of liberal media or conservative media outlets. It's almost like a handful of people censor and promote content based on what they want their news organizations to promote. This also goes into social media platforms. It's been proven that if a social media platform wants to promote let's say minority groups, then they magically receive more traffic than a normal post would.

VIDEO GAMES

Ooh, haven't video games become immersive over the years? I remember when we used to go to a pizza place and play Pac-Man on the table. Now, with VR first-person shooter headsets where you can practically lick the sweat off their faces, after you shoot them in the stomach. These games are immersive and they are incredible. You get lost for hours playing a game in virtual reality. Whether you're on your phone or playing with the new Xbox, the games have advanced over the years.

Video games are an extension of ourselves. They have an addictive quality, which can be detrimental if the addiction harms the child's development and desires. I've often considered how video games affect society and police interactions. The video games themselves inherently aren't bad; having your kid play them beats being a drug dealer on the street. However, the violent nature of video games will accentuate a curiosity to normalize that violence. Imagine playing the first-person shooter game continuously thinking that it's some normal behavior. This can train individuals to want to act out the very thing that they do for hours on end.

For a normal individual that has no desire to harm anyone, it's an innocent game. Yet it can become a catalyst for the individual who has the curiosity and desire to harm others. This alone is why video games could become harmful. It's the same for anything else. Many blame the gun for shooting people, but they forget that someone actually pulled the trigger. Guns don't kill people; people kill people. If you took away all the guns from law-abiding citizens, you'd still have criminals running around shooting people. The same goes for video games. You could remove all the video games, and the people who desire to harm others will find another way to get their motivation.

If you like to play video games or have a child that does, it's important to find yourself in the middle of the road with this immersive technology. Are they feeding the desire to harm others by playing this game? Or is it innocent fun they have every once in a while? There are always breadcrumbs with these things. More often than not, you're going to see some warning signs. In one case, an 18-year-old asked her parents if they could buy a gun out of nowhere. The mom said no to purchasing a gun and didn't inquire further. The 18-year-olds wanted to buy a gun because they determined they needed to end someone's life to protect them from someone else.

I'm not saying this situation could have changed entirely, but we can't avoid the warning signs, just like that third grader that brought a gun to school in Virginia. The teacher knew something was up, and they talked to the school about it; students reported it, and nobody did anything on multiple occasions. Later on, the teacher got shot by the six-year-old with the gun. If we see the warning signs, we need to do something about it.

This is where the parents need to step in and provide structure and accountability to their children. We can't wait until the kid dreams of killing somebody and goes to act on the dream because of the video games they've been playing. We have to have a culture in our homes that provides structure and accountability with our children so that we don't see them stray. With anything, including technology, we should deploy limits that are comfortable for the household. These boundaries should not be crossed with technology inside our homes. This generation will be the most technically savvy generation that is currently living; it is a blessing but equally a curse. Let's be mindful of the pros and cons of the day that we live in so we can see our families and ourselves down the road.

CHAPTER 6

What is going on in the brain?

OUR COGNITIVE PROCESSES ASSIST US IN EVERYTHING WE DO. Consciously or subconsciously, our actions are a derivative of our underlying brain function. Our brain responds differently, though, when it encounters stress. Those stress markers sometimes lead us to act irrationally because of their effects on our brains. More recently, I have spent much of my time helping people with their thoughts and ideas, helping them achieve new mindsets to assist them in their lives. It's easy to point out our behavior and say stop doing that, but if you don't change the foundation of that behavior, then you're just going to reproduce it. This prodded me into understanding the brain even more, first with policing because that's my background and the majority of people I help, and then secondarily with everyone else.

I want us to be more informed about controlling our bodies and behaviors and be mindful of heightened emotions and extreme behaviors that lead us to do harmful things. Also, let's look at some interesting dynamics that could contribute to increased stress. We should all understand how the brain functions and insert environments to be aware of the changes in our minds that affect our behavior.

BASIC BRAIN FUNCTIONS

Let's look at some of the brain's basic functions and how it affects us. Most of you have probably heard about the prefrontal cortex, the front part of the brain that gives us our intelligence. This part of the brain makes us smart and allows us to make logical, rational decisions. Then, we have the limbic system in a different area of the brain. This complex network of nerves controls the brain's emotional center. Anytime you have an emotion, it's primarily coming from the limbic system. We also have the amygdala, an almond-shaped mass inside the cerebral hemisphere involved in processing our emotions. Some also call the amygdala our fear center. The amygdala is also at the core of our autonomic nervous system, which controls bodily functions except for consequently directed functions such as breathing, heartbeat, and digestive process. It is involved in these basic functions changing according to stress levels.

When introduced to a highly stressful state, the amygdala kicks in, and our autonomic nervous system provides us with a fight, flight or freeze response. We discussed this idea briefly in previous chapters, but let's expound on it now. This response overrides our prefrontal cortex. It reduces or can even shut down our ability to have logical thought based on the automatic reactions/behaviors wired in the amygdala. So, if our fear or stress response is so great, parts of our brain are shut down, including our logical and rational areas. This brings people to a heightened stress point, much like someone being chased by a wild animal in the woods. What will they do, fall and play dead, start fighting the wild animal, or run as fast as possible?

This introduction to a fight, flight or freeze response is not subjugated to cavemen and cavewomen. We still have the same reactive brain system that our far back ancestors had. We all have this, and we must be mindful that our body does this in certain fear-induced states. There is an awesome example of fainting goats that tense their muscles so much that they fall over to the side and look like they are passing out when they encounter stress or fear. We do the same thing, just in a different way. Your choice to fight, fight or freeze is ingrained in your past and what your model is to do. If you grew up in a family of fighters and they always pushed back when they felt stressed, and they started fights, then you're more than likely going to fight when you feel fearful. You were trained to do that when you encounter fear and stress.

Our brain, when introduced to fear, is trying to protect us. Everything about its response is appropriate. We feel the fear, and our body is trying to kick in the appropriate action based on the fear that we are experiencing. The question is not about whether or not our body should be doing that; the question resides in our origin of that fear. On the one hand, we don't want to shut down the body's response to its stress receptors and ignore them. We want to be mindful when our body talks to us and informs us of something we should be hypervigilant and pay attention to. The problem resides in our origin of fear. When we're at a traffic stop because we were speeding, should we induce a level 10 fear response, 10 being the highest, equating to thinking we are about to die? Or, with proper understanding and process, we can be caught off guard by getting pulled over but not panicking and shut down the logical, rational side of our brain. If we induce a level 10 fear response, we will give our brain no other option but to fight, run away, or completely shut down. For those of you that have lived to fight or run away, you will be inviting some serious charges against you. In most cases that are questionable today with the police officers involving some form of threat of force or use of force, it is because the suspect started to fight the officers or run away from the officers. I'm not saying every case is like that; I'm just saying it seems most cases involve those two things.

Is it possible for us to avoid entering into the amygdala takeover zone and continue with logical, rational thought when we're in police encounters or when we are observing them? It's not just police interactions that I'm talking about; it's everything in life, but of course, when we're dealing with law enforcement. Too many of us seem to live in this fight, flight or freeze mode in life. It's not nearly as necessary in the 21st century. These days, we don't have that many threats coming into our life. Most of us wake up in a comfortable bed with heating and air conditioning. We go into our kitchen and get a bowl of cereal or make something for breakfast. Then we hop in our nice car and drive to work, where we sit behind a desk and stare at a computer all day. Maybe for lunch, we walked down the street to a local restaurant or brought our lunch from home. Then we drive home and plan to do the same thing the next day. That's not really the environment to enact our fight, flight, and freeze mode. As a basic human being, I believe that our brain is sometimes seeking out stress because we don't have enough of it in our lives.

We're interested in discussing dramatic events worldwide to make our lives more stress-filled. Our body craves confirmation of bias, and we'll have a heightened awareness to reaffirm any negative emotions we have. We watch the news on our phones and tell ourselves we're doing this to be informed, but we're actually seeking out stress. Our brain tells us we should know these things to protect us, but in reality, we could survive completely without knowing what happens with the news every day. Need another war update from the Middle East to make it through lunch? No. Do you need to know about the police chase that's happening right now in LA and how many people were involved? The answer is no, but we seek it out because we feel like we need to know.

There aren't many stressors in our life compared to life 100 years ago. That's why people like to do stress-filled activities. Have you ever seen people climb a rock face without a harness? Drive ridiculously fast? Or Instagrammers climbing on the top buildings without any safety gear? What about people that like to jump out of planes or bungee jump? All these people are seeking that emotion center in their brain to be activated. Do they want to die, or are they seeking out the stress that gives them a thrill?

Personally, I don't feel that being a cop is more dangerous than a lot of other things. I do not want to die in my profession. Statistically, you're way more likely to die as a construction worker in an accident than a police officer. The most dangerous job in America is being a logging worker. The number 22 most dangerous job in America is a police officer, behind mechanics and other construction jobs. Delivery drivers and pilots are way more likely to die at work than police officers. The police officers' threats are primarily accidents and criminal activity. Roughly half of all LEO's that die on the job are killed purposefully by another human. That is what makes the job different. I'm just trying to put policing into a new perspective for you.

Just because it's not the number one most dangerous job doesn't mean cops and civilians don't encounter that fear center when they meet. We are all still human and act continuously based on our fears and stressors. Police training does help to mitigate the complete takeover of our prefrontal cortex when we're under heightened stress. There is a basic idea of muscle memory for physical routines. Sports athletes live by this muscle memory. The brain functions in a similar fashion in that if you do something in a certain circumstance repeatedly, under stress the basic response is likely to occur. Routine kicks in, and we act on that routine along with the amygdala response. The one problem for law enforcement is they can't train for every situation. The same goes, however, for civilians, as I pointed out earlier. Should we practice proper coping strategies so we don't end up in fights with police officers? Obviously, police officers are going to be trained so they don't act instinctually when they encounter civilians. But they're only half of the equation, right?

When we seek out stress, we are given more stress continuously. When we click on links to articles that pertain to heightened stress elements our brain expects to see more of this stress induced content. Therefore we are provided with what we're seeking. We're told continuously now that police encounters are going wrong by the media, and that's because we seek out content like this. It doesn't mean it's more prevalent than anything else; it just means that's what we're deciding to digest more frequently. Guess what people are going to produce more often? Content that's engaging and that people look at. Whatever content can be stress-filled and provoke that emotion center in our mind will be fed to us.

So, in essence, we are training our brains every time we enact our fear center. That's how people can get to the conclusion of systematic problems. It feels like it's a systematic problem because that's the feeling that is taking over their brain. It's okay that we have feelings but don't want them. We don't want to teach our kids that their feelings are in charge of the situation. We want to teach our kids that feelings are messengers that tell us something about our mindsets or about our experiences. They're sending us a signal, and we should pay attention to that signal and see if we need to do anything to adjust the signal by solving it or if we need to change our minds. If we cater to our feelings continuously, we end up raising our kids in an environment without consequences. They're never allowed to have bad feelings. How long will we be able to protect our kids from their feelings? Until they're 25? No, we should assist them in processing their feelings and resolving them. That way, they have a better chance to grow up to be fantastic contributors to society and not terrible ones.

Jordan B. Peterson, a well known psychologist, says our number one responsibility as a parent is to ensure our children are socially acceptable by age four. If they're socially acceptable and others like them, they will learn how to manage relationships independently when they're older. They will be able to overcome difficulties and frustrations to maintain order, structure, and civility. They become an outcast if they're not liked or socially acceptable. Outcasts typically buck the system and fight whatever hierarchy they feel like is in charge. Ensuring they're socially acceptable is not the same as catering to them.

Dr. David Welch worked here in Minnesota. He is a psychologist who wrote the book, "No: Why children of all ages need to hear it, and ways parents can say it". He discusses brain development and boundaries. He discusses the brain with brain images and correlating stories. One of the obvious issues he brings up as a parent is inconsistent boundaries. If you have two kids who hit each other and the parent says no, don't hit, as they spank them. Then they also allow them to fight later. The proper behavior does not reinforce your no. You are demonstrating it's okay to hit and telling them they can hit sometimes. Your no is actually a yes because of what you have shown and it blurs the lines of acceptable behaviors and associated feelings.

What is wrong with kids and young adults having negative emotional feelings? It's healthy. It's very healthy. I'm not saying parents should create them. I know it sounds mean to teach them a lesson, but it's not. It happens in life; when it does, you can help your child deal with it. When our kids engage in "I want, I want, I want" communication, this is coming from the limbic system in their brain. This part of the neural network wiring is established when they were young and carries over to when they're adults. The incessant wanting can be a fear response to lack or scarcity. It may be cute when your kid is begging you for something, but imagine an 18-year-old with a fear of lack and scarcity; what will they do? Steal someone's purse because they want to buy something special for themselves? Are they willing to hurt someone else because they feel like they should have that girlfriend or boyfriend?

You'll probably see your child experience negative feelings when you say no. It may seem natural to try to alleviate your child from feeling those negative feelings, but you are removing them from having the ability to resolve their own emotions. You're taking away a vital component of their success if you try to solve their negative emotions for them when you say no to them hitting their sibling, or do you stick with your no and allow them to feel and see the consequences that come with it?

We want them to be independent thinkers who can provide their own solutions in life. As a parent, it isn't easy to switch between making decisions for your child and teaching them how to make decisions for themselves. It's a necessary one, though.

Don't let society tell you otherwise. We want to teach our kids to be open-minded and learn from their mistakes and that it's okay to experience different kinds of emotions and go through the process of understanding what that means and the consequences of those actions.

We are in a constant state of pursuing happiness, and we don't want to let anyone down. That's when every kid in the classroom gets a number one trophy because we don't want anyone to feel like they got second place. What does that do? It teaches our kids there are no consequences and there are no repercussions with action. There's no opportunity for them to learn anything from their mistakes. If this continues and is exacerbated into adulthood, they may likely feel like they can steal from others and harm others without consequence. When they encounter law enforcement because of their terrible actions, they act out and are surprised because someone's trying to hold them accountable. A lot of today's policing is done because of poor parenting. Ask any law enforcement officer and I'm sure they can share with you at least one, if not many instances of a mid 20's or 30-something under arrest crying and screaming for their mommy.

It's hard to say, but it's true. Our parents set us up to succeed in life or fail because our parents provide us with a blueprint for living our lives. They're not solely responsible for our actions but do contribute. How we interact with our kids replicates how they could engage in society. If we have police encounters and we're respectful to the officers, what will our children see? If we follow the law, how are our children likely to act when they encounter something in the future? Will they obey a lawful order or decide it's a perfect time to defy and fight the police officer? We can train our brains to respond to these situations differently.

There is a TV show called the Alaskan Frontier, and everything they do requires a heightened stress level. If you're fishing for your food, you'll be anxious and stressed because you may not catch anything. You may also have to fend off other animals trying to eat your food or eat you. When you sleep on the cot or on the floor of your cabin; you don't know if you're going to get bit by something or if you might get frostbite when you wake up in the morning. When you cut down firewood, you're trying to avoid getting hit by a tree. When you drink water out of the creek, you don't know if there are bacteria in there, and you might die. We are likely just seeking out stress/drama filled TV shows because our easy, technology driven life doesn't have enough stress in it. Even the Alaskan Frontier shows may provide us with the drama we need, not just the Kardashians or Jersey Shore. People seek out TV shows like this because they activate our brains' stress centers.

My grandfather was born in 1898, and he loved watching All-Star wrestling in the 70's before the sport admitted it was fake. Even when I was young, I knew it was fake, but boy, he would turn on the fear center in his brain and scream at the TV. His emotions would get so charged watching All-Star wrestling. It was insane. Even though the show was probably scripted, he would enact his natural instinct and get worked up. We do the same thing with our vices. Maybe we could do a little less of it because it's changing the chemical makeup of our brains. My advice, stop looking for things to activate the limbic system, or recognize that you are doing it and find your own personal stressors like rock climbing without ropes. By the way, the Park Rangers or area law enforcement that find you after you fall will appreciate your stress management skills... not!

INTELLIGENCE QUOTIENT (IQ)

Our IQ also contributes to our decision-making. The standard IQ is about 100. Most people in the US are in the range of 73 -113 and on one end of the spectrum, you have people that are extremely smart and have an IQ of 145 or more. They would be on the right side of the extreme. Brilliant people have IQs of 145 or higher. In most cases, their increased IQ leads to increased effectiveness in life, and they can produce tremendous things that very few others would even consider.

On the low end of the IQ perspective, some people are in their 70s, 60s, and 50s. That is a very low IQ, and even the military has standardization to what kind of IQ they accept. This level of IQ can contribute to many unfortunate things. Our in-depth decision-making, and our IQ coupled with our EQ (emotional intelegence) leads to either positive or tremendously negative interactions. Unfortunately, people with low IQs and extremely low IQs lead to more police confrontations because they're not able to think complexly and manage their emotional state during these encounters. That's why cops undergo many hours of training specifically geared to how to deal with people with cognitive disorders and disabilities, including low IQ. There aren't any real solutions to this presently available apart from awareness.

HAPPINESS

Happiness is something we all should have access to. It's not a replacement for all the other areas of emotion we should experience, but it's definitely a goal. In the early 80s, they studied the happiest place on Earth and found it was somewhere in southern Mexico. It was a poor town where people lived in shacks and their happiness had nothing to do with prosperity or money. The crime was low, and people were nice to each other. At the end of a hard work day, they have a beer and play cards or go to the beach. They didn't care about Mercedes or Chevy or their house's size. Everything they had was minimal, so their happiness could be greater. They eliminated many of their problems and largely disconnected themselves from the rest of the world; therefore, they weren't influenced by the world's problems. Of course the internet has drastically changed this.

Pursuing happiness should be done with the utmost amount of responsibility and avoiding artificial stressors. We shouldn't pursue stress as much just because our brain craves it. We should retrain our brain to appreciate when things aren't stressful and when we're not reading or watching something stressful. We should appreciate the peace at the moment that comes out of us, taking responsibility for our actions and our mind.

CHAPTER 7

Government

Growing up in the United States is probably one of the most free environments that exists in the world. America is only a couple hundred years old, and it was established on some really advanced, progressive principles to protect the individual and accelerate their life. Part of the construct of the American way and its ideals comes from its correlation to all of the bad ideals that it had to overcome. Countries are formed around ideals and principles to live by. There's no country like the United States because of its benefits and freedoms. I can write this book under the premise of having free speech. People can go out on the streets and hold rallies around their ideas. They have protections, and their interests are protected in those systems. That is the true benefit to our culture established in the bedrock of our government.

By no means is the United States perfect, and perhaps it doesn't desire to be. Individual freedoms are emphasized in their uniqueness versus perfection. Everyone's life, liberties, and the pursuit of happiness are the priority, not just your life, liberty, and the pursuit of happiness. It's also your neighbors. This creates the ultimate conundrum for those that are not open and accepting of others. I have to live with my neighbor next door. He or she may have different thoughts about how to live their life. That is the American dream. We agree to that tension that could exist within those freedoms. That's what makes us great. What am I to do when my neighbor does something that offends me? Should they be taken away, never to be seen again? Or should we find civil ways to agree to disagree and move on with life? Live and let live.

But this doesn't mean we don't have standards. Of course, we have standards, and where our standards lie, that's where the laws come from. Our interpretation of those laws and enforcement of those laws is what makes us a country. If we have an erosion of those things that make us who we are today, we will migrate from the foundation of what makes our country succeed. Depending on what political parties lead the government at the time determines what kind of laws will be enacted and how they would be enforced. Everything is perfectly fine if people are held accountable for their behaviors attached to enforceable laws. If they're no longer held accountable for their behaviors, then society's threads fall apart.

With those great advantages, we also have the disadvantages of such freedoms. If people could speak their minds because of the right to free speech, then they would surely be offended by what others have to say. If people can bear arms and protect their families, surely there are going to be people that will feel unsafe because others have guns in their possession. There's always a juxtaposition to the great advantages that we have. The only way we find harmony in the middle of that tension is with how we enforce today's laws and regulations with the backbone of structure and the sensitivity of the moment.

We don't want to trample on people's rights but maintain some sort of balance amid the chaos. That's exactly what law enforcement provides. They hold the scales of justice and personal rights and try to find the balance amid the craziest circumstances people find themselves in. If you were to remove or inhibit this vital component, then you would end up with lawlessness or complete control from the government. It's easy to see these two options displayed in other countries.

There are some countries where you're not allowed to use the internet freely and in other countries where women aren't allowed to drive cars or hold any meaningful job. There are countries today with active slaves, and there are severely impoverished countries that don't have the means for the future because of how their government handles their affairs. Are we open to relinquishing our freedoms so our government can handle all of our affairs? Or should we understand the government's role and maximize our personal responsibility for our own lives? I believe it's the latter. As a former police officer, law enforcement has a clear role today. It's evident, and it's clearly needed. Nevertheless, I won't rely on police officers to raise my kids. That's my job, not somebody else's.

So, on the one hand, I see the value in our governmental institutions and how they provide us with context and a framework for how we can live our lives and pursue life, liberty and happiness. For that, I'm grateful and proud to be an American. I feel people get it wrong because they tie into political notions that lead them away from the pursuit of life, liberty, and happiness. They look at the extremes of every situation and try to create conflict where there isn't any. Generally speaking, what do people have to complain about? Grow up, care for your family, get a good job, and enjoy your life. It seems like drama and conflict are created out of nowhere for the sake of divisiveness.

THE TREND OF DIVISIVENESS

Whether you are political or not, the government affects your life in one way or another. Some like to acknowledge the government's influence in our lives daily, while others ignore those realities. Nevertheless, our government has a direct say in how we go about our life and what we should or shouldn't be doing regularly. This ties back to the tension that we have with our laws. We elect our officials and enact laws based on peer consensus. The people you live next to and what they believe have a direct say on how your community will develop.

In the 1960s, I grew up hearing of Martin Luther King Jr. I believe he's probably rolling over in his grave right now looking at the separation and divisiveness that's used in his name. He stood for unity and connection that looked at the heart of humanity, and pursued ways to remove the intellectual barriers that kept people from loving each other. Today, we see a reintroduction of divisiveness and separation, especially in our liberal movements, to gain some political agenda. People are put at odds with each other over what I believe are largely non-issue ideas. This is ultimately the harm that a government can bring when one political party villainizes the other for the sake of their personal gain rather than the holistic thriving of everyone. Isn't America supposed to be a melting pot? That means we melt and combine, not stay hard and separate.

This is most evident in politics, where someone has the opportunity to gain power and money in some way or another. If you step back and look at the policies enacted in the last 20 years, every one of them will be time for some financial component. Whether it be wars in Iraq or Afghanistan, big pharma and vaccines for everyone, or Barack Obama's solar initiatives and green energy and carbon emissions, every single one of these initiatives has huge budgets that feed into the engine of political reciprocity through the association. It's scary to think about how politicians are empowered by their choices through this cycle versus caring first about those that elected them.

It seems the only way for one party to create the absolute and extreme narratives is to make an 'All or Nothing' argument. This leaves no negotiation of free will or a gray area amid the 'All or Nothing' choice. You're either with us or against us on every issue. This can be seen across the board. Not only is it toxic, it creates wild agendas that are extreme on every front. Divisiveness actually becomes the goal because there needs to be a clear juxtaposition. If we don't absolutely disagree, then we might be perceived as agreeing, and nothing will get done for my party. It's great to have many ideas, but they need to be facilitated in a way that provides a healthy foundation for progress instead of putting people at odds with each other.

We should be alarmed and push back if we're required to disregard the opinions of our neighbors for the sake of political affiliation. People are more important than political parties; at the end of the day, we're all human, so we should be able to find reasonable common ground on every issue. For example, If you have a restaurant and want your patrons to be able to smoke, it's legal to smoke. Then who's to tell you you can't allow people to smoke in your restaurant? Should the government tell you that even though it's legal to smoke, you can't smoke while you're in a restaurant?

If people don't want to be around smoke, they don't have to go to the restaurant. Right? Shouldn't a restaurant owner be allowed to conduct their business how they see fit within the confines of the current of people being allowed to smoke in their state? I see it from both sides, but I disagree with the government's overreach in this particular case. If it's legal to smoke, you should be able to smoke where you want. If a restaurant doesn't want people to smoke in it, that's their choice. I say all this even though I don't smoke. If you think that smoking should be illegal, then vote for it. Otherwise, we, the government, should stay the heck out of it.

One of the latest political tools to create divisiveness is data manipulation or selective illumination. See, facts tell a story. That story is the narrative that the political party has to go off of. When you receive data, your arguments are dispelled or substantiated. You're either reinforcing the ideas you believe to be true, or you have to change your ideas because the facts don't align. Imagine you have a hundred data points and decide to build an argument around three of them. They are inherently true because there are three data points, but it's not the full picture. It's a partial picture of personal gain versus truth and transparency. We see this evident in our government and across the board in the media. It's only to create reinforced narratives and divisiveness. We should be mindful of these tactics that are used daily so we don't fall prey to them.

LOWEST COMMON DENOMINATOR

The thing that screams the loudest gets the most attention. Unfortunately for the collective, they are largely ignored. The government often caters to the most emotionally charged ideas and people. Hear me out for a second. I'm not saying that because someone has emotions means they're the least common denominator. I'm saying if you're in a room with 100 people and 99 of them are being quiet, and one person stands up and starts screaming something; the 99 people have to wait patiently until the one person calms down for everyone to proceed. This is an analogy of how our government approaches the political enforcement of its ideas.

If one person is making enough noise, they carry the engagement at that moment. This doesn't mean we re-engineer our focus around those things that actually need help and attention. This means we focus on the things that scream at us. So instead of looking at child poverty and nutrition or homelessness in some cases, we are focused on all the new kinds of genders that are being created every day and transgender rights in women's sports. Our government tells us to focus on sexuality in children's curriculum and whether the NFL can pray before its games. Whatever is screaming the loudest gets attention versus the things that actually make a difference.

The education system is a reflection of this ideal. If you take a classroom of 10 kids and the majority are not doing well on their test scores, then you change the grading system to accommodate those not doing well. The introduction of the curve grading system allows those failing to get by with passing grades because their classmates didn't score the highest scores in the class. It removes the standard from 100 to the average. Does this create a more educated society or an erosion of standards for people not to be offended or held back? Keep Up People!

The erosion of systems brings us to detrimental places. In some cities, so many kids wouldn't qualify to graduate that the city changed its criteria for them to graduate rather than being held back because they didn't have room for all these kids to be held back another year. (No child left behind - Thanks George W. Bush) The system that I grew up with was an A was 100%, and anything below 60% was an F. An F was synonymous with failing. You would be held back if you failed the class that was required. Several schools recently adopted policies that eliminated D's and F's from their grading practices. This is called a no-fail policy. The student would start at a 55% score and only need to accumulate 5% to graduate. The grading system was thrown out the window for an acceptable versus an unacceptable grade.

If a student received an A or B, they would be given that grade, and everyone else would be given the grade of Pass. Why would they go through such trouble? It was because students were failing at such a high rate in the middle of the semester, that they knew that some minority groups would fall drastically behind if they couldn't graduate. In 2020 the percentage of failed classes among Latino high school students was 24.9%; for Black high school students, it was 23.2%. This compares with 12.9% for white students and 7.6% for Asians. The idea was that they would fall behind in life because they couldn't graduate with the premise for all the rule changes. Does it actually help them in life, though? If they can't complete the standard education, how can they succeed as an adult and be contributing members of society? Now let's think about the fact that kids aren't held accountable as we progress through the years. Is this helping?

This is the problem that we face today. It's not that we don't have the right systems or laws in place for us to have a productive and constructive society; it's that word changing how we enforce those systems to accommodate the least common denominator. My suggestion would be that we hold to our standards and find out what we need to do to bring people up to the standard of excellence necessary for them to live a great life and for them to be productive and contribute to our communities, versus changing the enforcement of our standards in order to not offend people and hold them back because they didn't pass the standardized tests. Are we really helping people by pushing them along and giving them a pat on the back for failing? If we have the standards, then why not enforce them? What's the point of having standards if they don't matter? This is the slow erosion of a great country. Does everyone truly deserve a trophy for existing? I think this simple concept of not offending anyone or making them feel bad is inherently detrimental to growth and perseverance. We need to see what success and failure look like to create a target and a goal in our mind on what to achieve, versus allowing everything to be permissible. Our children especially need to see what is good versus bad for them to achieve greatness. As a parent, it's so hard not to come down and do everything for your children, but ultimately, we are handicapping their growth if we don't have standards to achieve and standards to live by.

https://www.latimes.com/california/story/2020-12-14/lausd-extend-no-fail-policy-january-covid-19

WE THE PEOPLE

When most people think of the government, their first thought is about politicians. This should not be the case. We should think first about our rights and our views being expressed through our government. We, the people, should be how we approach the views of our government. The government should express our views, how we want to be governed, taxed, and what we see as permissible in our lives. We affect change by hosting conversations amongst ourselves and sharing our ideas and differences openly.

Suppose we're thinking first about sustainability and what creates a thriving environment. In that case, we will bring people together and host these conversations and not let political narratives get in the way of what we see as life, liberty, and the pursuit of happiness. The idea of change comes when we start to adopt responsibility. The right and privilege to adopt change on a governmental level comes when we vote and who we vote for. Their thoughts and beliefs will affect your life more than you know. If you care about safe environments, then make sure you vote for someone in office that will provide the means for that on a local, state, and federal level. You choose the world you want to live in based on the people you elect in office.

Lastly, we are all human; we need to be together on our issues and work on them alongside each other. It is not I, the people, but we, the people, that bring about the best. I believe it's what Martin Luther King Jr wanted. He wanted to bring people together to create the best, and that's what we should do today. So regardless of your political affiliations, find common ground and build on top of that to create something that's sustainable for the future.

CHAPTER 8

Drama

WE ALL HAVE REAL STRESS IN OUR LIFE. Waking up in the morning and thinking to yourself, do I have enough food to eat? If you drive to the store to get food, an appropriate amount of stress goes into awareness, making sure you don't run into someone. Once you've arrived at the store and to buy something, you have to decide if you can afford it. Perhaps these examples are mild, but they can be severe depending on your situation, and they are real stressors in our life. If you're rich like Paris Hilton or Warren Buffett, perhaps you have someone make breakfast and buy everything you need at the store. Even rich people have stress about their Investments and finances. They just have more zeros to think about.

Even if you're not rich, you can just have stuff sent to your house, remove potential stressors like driving, and have everything delivered. You may even have a job where you work from home, or you're retired. On a day-to-day basis, the stress level we encounter is quite mild compared to what it used to be 100 years ago and beyond. Back in the day, there were genuine concerns about whether or not there was enough food to eat or adequate shelter from the elements. Most would fear getting some type of sickness or disease because healthcare was mostly non-existent. The typical lifespan was significantly impacted based on these very present realities. They had very real stress for all the right reasons.

Looking at homelessness in America for the last decade, it never reached a level of 1% of the population, or 500K out of 300 million. Within the total homeless population, over 60% of them have some type of alternative housing that they stay at. That doesn't mean there's not a problem. It just means that over 99% of Americans have somewhere to sleep at night.

Also, according to the CDC, about 14,000 Americans each year die of starvation. Of course, a very large percentage of people have some type of nourishment insecurity. However, 99% of Americans have food to eat every day. so it's safe to say that most Americans have mild stressors in their life. Of course, there are always individual unique examples where people have very stressful lives, but on the whole, I'm talking about the majority, and everybody lives pretty much a stress-free life. Let's evaluate a few ways where we self-induce stress and why.

FINDING WAYS TO INDUCE STRESS

Our predictable lives actually have very few true stressors. So how do we fix this and find ways to introduce stress in our lives? Our brains are wired to keep us alive, so they're fixated on anything that could be negative so that we avoid dying. If you put two options in front of me, one of them could threaten my life, and the other is good news, guess which one I'm going to pick. The first one, of course, was the one that could threaten my life. This brings us to the common American who finds ways to induce stress in their life.

We wake up, read the news and the torld report about all the terrible things that took place last night and this week. We find out who died recently and what major political threat is happening in our state and government. This gets us riled up and agitated about the day because we can't believe what half of the country is doing and how crazy the world is. Throughout the day, we see breaking news alerts, riots, wars and death somewhere thousands of miles away. If there's not something breaking that day, then it will be a rerun from the previous week to keep us engaged and stressed.

We finish up our work day, and it's finally time to rest with our families, and we decide to put on a movie. For some, their tea is reality tv, like Desperate Housewives or Bridezilla. Lots of people like watching the Kardashians. In one episode, they're trying to decide if they will buy something that's 8 or 10 carats. No one can relate to that on any realistic scale. Then they get into a fake argument over a relationship or which car they should drive. It doesn't provide any substitute value to our lives. However, we turn it on, and we watch them argue for 45 minutes, and we can't wait to do it again next week when the new episode comes out.

For others, like me, I put on an action film that could include war, crime, or a battle against good and evil. We watch it because it keeps us engaged, a framework in our mind that looks for and is addicted to these stressful events. If you were to ask common people why they watch certain things, they would tell you that they like it. Perhaps, their liking it means their brain is attracted to it, which could inevitably be the stress response kicking in and wiring the brain around things to avoid. I like watching movies like Saving Private Ryan because I associate it with the service and the Act of Valor. I appreciate the storyline and the lessons that come from movies like that. I look for brotherhood, camaraderie, and sacrifice, and those are the things that I'm attracted to watching. It helps bring some sense of meaning to my life of service. When I see those characteristics, it makes me feel good and stimulates me to want to watch more of these kinds of movies.

Some like watching unrealistic science fiction. The movies where future realities, aliens and far-off lands are discovered, explored, and developed, like Star Wars. If there's any present drama, the brain's fear center will be activated. I'm not an expert in drama, but I know our fear centers turn on whenever we see a conflict. When there's a galactic war going on, or someone's about ready to lose their oxygen tank in the middle of space. Your fear centers are kicking in and making you focus intently to ensure you don't do the same thing to yourself.

Extreme and exacerbated media is meant to keep our attention, but rarely gives us any true value or benefit. Today, influencers, TV personalities, actors, and actresses are taught to engage the emotional centers in our brains to keep us focused on them and their messages. Our awareness is half the battle because most people don't even know what's happening to them. They don't know why certain commercials work, and they don't know why certain movies or TV shows always keep them interested.

Continually focusing on stress-related media induces unnecessary stress that's plaguing our minds. We don't know any better when we're in the moment because that's what our brain is telling us that it wants, but is it the best thing for us? Always seeking out drama increases the cortisol that flows through our body, inevitably affecting our physical well-being and health. It can also retrain our brains to want more of this useless drama. This is the true demise of media and algorithms, where people are fed a continual stream of stress-induced content because we are prone to search it out to protect us, thus creating a bad cycle that's hard to break.

Imagine walking down the sidewalk, and across the street, you see two people getting into a fight. Very few of you could walk away without letting it affect you. Most of you would stop and watch because it's magnetic to our brains. We have to see it play out, and we need to follow it through the end. It's just like a good movie. The crazy thing is, if we didn't care to watch the fight playing out across the street and we ignored it because it didn't matter to us, then would we actually be preventing future fights because nobody cares to see them? Actually, yes, we would.

WHAT IS THE PURPOSE

The thing we focus on and give our attention to is the thing that increases in our life. If people realize they're receiving attention and affirmation for something they're doing, whether it's good or bad, they will increase that to amplify the attention they're getting. If I act like a crazy lunatic, I will get people's attention. When people watch me and continue to rewatch me, acting like a lunatic, they are celebrating me. We need to be mindful of this when we seek out drama and things that are stress-inducing.

We will never be able to fully stop this drama-seeking response in our brain because it's there to protect us. However, the more we become mindful of these events and episodes where we're caught in the loop of drama-filled needless stress consumption, we can snap out of it and tell ourselves it's okay to let that go and give our cognitive abilities a break or entertain them with something that would benefit us or educate us. Remove yourself from the breaking news alert notifications and the urgent email notifications you're probably signed up for. If you check the news continuously throughout the day, delete the app or ask yourself why you are on here. What are you ultimately looking for? If you can't come up with a legitimate reason for checking the news cycle six times a day, you need to help curb your addiction.

When I was working directly in law enforcement, I would get off of a stressful shift and participate in mindless activities. I would avoid anything that would trigger my stress responders, like watching the news or following up on a court case. Most cops play video games to keep their minds off of things. I'm constantly looking for and trying to tell people to find the purpose in what they are giving so much of their precious time and thoughts to. If you don't have a purpose, why are you doing something?

If reading an article aims to increase the overall awareness and betterment of one's understanding, then that's great. If your purpose for reading an article is because of habit, will it benefit you? I would ask you to consider your purpose in drama-related activities as advancing your life or just feeling a meaningless void of stress-induced activities. Ask yourself what you are seeking out and whether it's bringing you short-term and long-term benefits. I would challenge you to reconsider those drama-filled activities that activate the stress center of the brain because it can change the trajectory of your thought life and your body drastically.

HOW DOES THIS DRAMA-FILLED LIFE SPILL OUT INTO THE STREETS?

Society is a construct of individuals acting out what they see in their own minds. Suppose we gather together a bunch of people that have continuously unnecessarily induced stress in their minds because of the things they think about, watch, and obsess over. How does this affect our neighborhoods, communities, workplaces, police interactions, and ultimately our country? It's hard not to say that it affects us in tremendous ways. We're going to carry the level of cortisol and stress-induced responses into our everyday lives.

Our normal interactions may involve an extra dose of fight, flight, or freeze. This is very alarming especially given the increase in domestic abuse and police interactions. Suppose one is continuously filling their mind with heightened anxiety and stress levels. In that case, people will find themselves at a breaking point more frequently and more severely than in the previous season. Including unnecessary drama is not just a fun talking point, but it's critical for society to understand. I believe there's a direct correlation between one's individual stress-induced state and how it spills over into society.

Think about this concept with me for a minute. If you live in a high crime area like the south side of Chicago where shootings happen every single day, how would that affect your life, actions, and brain? You would probably carry a higher level of continual stress. That's a given. With that continued level of stress, you'd probably be on edge with people more frequently than someone in a city that didn't have as many shootings. You'd probably associate people dying on the street with something that is normal because it's normal for you because it happens every day, and you just have to live with it. It may affect your sleep and your ability to think about the future because you could die tomorrow if a bullet goes in the wrong direction. See, many get caught in this trap and think about partnering with this level of violence because it's the only way to protect themselves. Our environments drastically dictate the level of stress that we may be encountering. Again, our environments are simply a collection of individuals, and what they think is displayed on the streets daily.

COME BACK TO REALITY!

Sometimes the drama gets to us. What do I mean by that? We actually start to believe whatever story or narrative is being told to us. Whether it's systemic racism without a factual basis or it's your fourth-grade teacher telling you that everybody in this classroom can become an astronaut if they want to. I don't want to crap on anybody's dreams because it's fantastic to have dreams, but how much of what we think and obsess over is closer to reality?

I saw a pole that came out a while back about questions they asked white and black male kids. The pole asked black kids in elementary school what they would like to do when they grow up. 90% of the black kids said they wanted to play football or basketball and have a million-dollar job. 10% of the black kids said they wanted to be a doctor, a firefighter, an electrician, or any other kind of job unrelated to sports. Then they pulled the white male kids and asked them the same question. What do you want to do when you grow up? 90% of the white male kids said they wanted to be a doctor, a firefighter, or an electrician, all unrelated to sports. Only 10% of the white male kids said they wanted to be in some professional sport.

There is a huge difference in response between white and black male kids. Let's look at this statistically and see what probability their dreams and aspirations are tied to. Let's look at the NFL, for example, as it's one of the primary professional sports that black males aspire to go into. At any one time, 16,000 college-age kids are draft eligible, which is only 1.6% of the entire college pool. Out of the 16,000, only 259 players will be drafted each year. That is a tiny 0.016% of the draft-eligible NCAA pool. Those stats are from draft eligible NCAA college students. If we look at the number of kids that aspire to go into the NFL but don't make it through college or even go, the percentage is even worse. Every year 3.7 million people graduate high school.

Let's say 50% of the 3.7 million were males. That's 1.85 million males who graduate every year and have a .00014% chance of being drafted into the NFL. Wow! That's not very likely. I'm not just wanting to rain on everybody's parade; I want to bring about mindfulness and the dreams and aspirations we tell our kids they're allowed to have.

Of course, there's an idea that you could become anybody you'd like to be, but after a simple assessment of your DNA, skill sets, access to funds, and education, that should give you a more predictable path. Only some people are six foot seven and run a 4-minute mile. What's the best thing we should do for our kids? Should we allow them to dream and fantasize about something that is very unlikely, like a .00014% chance? Or should we help them perfect their interests and desires into something more attainable?

Imagine a child today who thinks that they will be in the NFL. Now, when I say child, I'm not talking about a 6 year old. Please don't think I believe we should squash the dreams of little children. I'm talking more about how their dreams unfold as they turn 11 or 14. How much of their life will they live, work, and dream around making it big one day rather than working at something diligently and developing a skill or craft that helps them immediately? How many children are left stuck without a reasonable alternative to making it in the NFL and resulting in trying to make it big by doing something else like selling drugs or stealing? If you have this idea that someone will pick you out of nowhere and you're going to become a millionaire, you will find an association with that premise for the rest of your life. Most kids out of high school don't automatically become a millionaire unless they sell drugs or go to the NFL. 99.9% of us must continually work hard and build our wealth over time.

The best thing we can do is tie our children into something obtainable and actionable. Cultivate their dreams and test things out by exploring what they can do today that they can carry into their future. I'm going to say that we all know, but none of us would want to say it, we all can't be in the NFL, or become astronauts, or NBA stars. Even if the movies tell us that we can and the bedtime stories say that you can be anybody you want to be, that's not actually reality. I knew I would never play in the NBA because I wasn't built for it. I found a career I liked and was passionate about that I could retire with. You probably came to a similar conclusion, and I hope you can lead your kids on that path as well. The path of the most realistic so that their expectations are set up, and they can build momentum in their life.

CHAPTER 9

Mindfulness Techniques

LET'S EXPLORE THE PRACTICAL SIDE of what I spend most of my time doing: helping cops in therapy. Everything I do in my practice can be applied to the general public. I see a mutually beneficial understanding that comes with some tools I've helped create and borrowed through the years. In some big or small way, I want this book to impact you, your family, and your community. That impact may come through perspective and paradigm shifts, and it might also come from practical tools like the ones I'm about to show you.

In basic terms, mindfulness is what you pay attention to. In therapy, you may exchange one idea for another. where you take negative emotion and exchange it for a more positive one. In my practice, I teach mindfulness techniques based on the desired outcome. Mindfulness is about paying attention to you. One of the ways to be mindful is to pay attention to your feelings and your perceptions. You look at them critically, and you separate yourself from them. Mindfulness is not simply about the facts; it's not simply about the feelings entirely, and it's not even about the lens through which you see the situation. It's a neutral big picture.

Imagine being at a concert with 300 people. Every single person has a different perspective on the situation. Every single person feels a particular way. Every person has a different approach to their desired outcome. One of the primary goals of mindfulness techniques is to see the world with neutrality and remove yourself from its focal point. If we realize that all 300 people have different experiences, we might open our minds to the potential experiences and outcomes that could happen.

The concert is more of a societal example. Everyone makes life about them. Some people can't incorporate anyone else into their thoughts or perspective. My rights, my body, my choice, me me, me, me. I'm not saying individual rights and choices are bad; I'm proposing a mindfulness technique that includes everyone. There will be no debate for me about whether or not people have individual rights and choices. However, the tension of this lesson is for the individual to decide if they can exercise the perspective that includes other people. It does not make their individual process void, but expands it into something greater. Now, their rights are coupled with the person's rights to their left and right, their bodies, and their choice. It's such a subtle change, but such a drastic result.

When I first exercised this, I felt like my brain was stretching. My natural process would be to return to my original thoughts and exclude everyone else because it feels way more comfortable. Even though I know it's right to include others in my thought processes, it still feels uncomfortable sometimes. What benefit do I have in seeing the world through their perspective and mine? This was one of the frequently asked in my therapy sessions. How are they helping me? I guess it always goes back to what we care about, and realize that our goals include them. Therefore, I can't ignore what makes us uncomfortable, but rather, we have to figure out the change we need to make for our lives to have harmony.

Situations in life bring us to need these mindfulness techniques. Cops tell me all the time when they're patrolling the streets, people talk about their first amendment right to be a ******. They say they can talk however they want to police officers with no recourse. They have the right to be an ******. That is true. They do have the right to be an a******. However, if they choose to be an a******, then they should expect to be treated like one. Now, this may come as quite a problem for the person who's choosing to be an a******. How could someone treat me the same way that I'm treating them? That's not fair. I reserve the right to treat people like crap, but expect them to treat me amazingly. That's not how life works. There's a beautiful thing called reciprocity. You always get what you give out. Can you see within this situation how the individual who's treating the police officer like an a****** would receive an equal response? Of course, I would hope all police officers are acting professionally and not lowering their standards to meet some unappreciated a******. However, they are people. Should you treat your mother that way? Would you say those same things to the person at Chick-fil-A? How about family members? This was a way too relatable exercise. As a matter of fact, it happens all the time.

Mindfulness techniques help us to do exercises that stretch our brains with the hope and intention that we will see the bigger picture. Somehow we begin to see beyond ourselves and see things how others see them. I would need to practice some form of mindfulness technique when I was doing traffic stops. I would pull someone over for running a stop sign. I would start talking to them and ask them questions about their intent to run the stop sign. I would say things like, did you know that you ran a stop sign back there? I would check to see if they're giving me any signs of remorse. I know they ran through the stop sign, but will they own their mistake or willful disobedience of a lawful directive?

One time I stopped a woman for a stop sign violation, and I approached her and started talking to her about it. She started cussing back at me and complaining. After a while, I stopped her from speaking and asked her to exit the car. I said, step out here; look back there. Do you see where you ran the stop sign right there, two blocks away? Immediately, she sees the stop sign and is filled with remorse. She goes, oh my God, I never saw it. I'm so sorry. I'm just now seeing this. I'm so sorry; she started tearing up for being such a b**** to me. After seeing her genuine response, I realized that she had learned her lesson; therefore, I didn't need to give her a ticket.

After great hesitation, she stepped outside her perspective and saw things the way I saw things for that moment in time. She wanted to continue to be a productive member of society and genuinely felt bad that she could have hurt someone by running the stop sign. The city put it there to ensure that a driver has a meaningful stop to ensure that they won't run into anyone else and to allow other traffic to commence. Once she saw the same thing that I saw, we connected on a level of genuine honesty. I've also had many traffic stops that went the other way. Where people acted like assholes, and there's no way I'm not going to give them a ticket because I couldn't leave with them thinking their attitude got them out of their responsibility for obeying the law. I was sure not to give them a break after how they treated me.

Trust me, after my decades of experience, being a jerk never gets you out of a ticket if a cop is pulling you over because of an observed behavior, like running a stop sign. Your process and communication with the police officer will let them know that you care, your intent, and your cooperation. You may have broken the law, and they have the right to issue you a ticket. If you deserve it, then own it. Accept the ticket and deal with it. This goes for cops giving other cops tickets as well. If you did break the law, then by all means, you should expect the penalty that goes with it. The silver lining is if we treat people with respect and we're honest, then perhaps we get away with the benefit of the doubt in the midst of some of our mistakes. The best part is that we're not trying to get worked up and create more problems than we already have. The responsibility and ownership that the driver shows during these stops are correlated to the willingness to adopt someone else's perspective. Can they dig down inside their emotions for a moment amid a traffic stop and see it from someone else's perspective? For those that do, they tend to have more favorable outcomes.

PAYING ATTENTION

One of the techniques I like to teach other police officers is imaging, which focuses on paying attention to yourself, asking yourself questions, and arguing with yourself. Men's and women's brains are different, which is scientifically proven through functional brain imaging. We now know that males' and females' brains operate differently. Women tend to be much better at multitasking. One of the best examples is the form of a conversation. You get a group of men together. Generally, one guy talks at a time. You get a group of women together, and they seem to all be talking simultaneously and listening. Men seem to have a more difficult time tracking multiple conversations at once, while women do it more easily. The point is that everyone's brain operates differently.

In my office, I have observed that men tend to have a less

utilized limbic system that tracks emotions. I often ask emotional-based questions like, How does that make you feel? How did that feel emotionally? The most common response is," It sucks" I said, Okay, I get it but "sucks" is not an emotion. What emotions come up for you? One client goes. Oh yeah. Okay, I get it. And he sat there, quiet for a while he went. Well, you know. It's just not cool. I said cool is a temperature rating. What emotion did you feel?

He couldn't come up with one. He says I don't know what you mean. So I go, okay. I was avoiding this, but I'm like, does it make you happy, sad, horny, hungry, or embarrassed. What emotion? He said it makes me sad. He borrowed one of my examples, because he couldn't identify one independently.

I realized at this moment that many people have a tough time recalling and communicating true emotions from a place of self-reflection. One of the core ways to grow in yourself is by paying attention to yourself. Get in your head a little and ask yourself questions about your thoughts, feelings, and intent. The better we ask ourselves questions, the better we will be around others. If necessary, argue with yourself. Speak to yourself loudly in your own mind and see how you respond. As you continue to talk and argue with yourself, you will start developing your solutions, coping strategies, and answers. You may realize that venting to yourself is way more productive than involving others sometimes. You solved your emotions and didn't let it spill out into a future conversation.

THE COIN FLIP

An extension of arguing with yourself is commonly referred to as the coin flip. We all have some sort of bend politically to think one way or another. We've got strong ideas about certain topics that emotionally move us to think a certain way. The question is whether or not we're open to considering what the rest of the world thinks and why. I've had some friends that travel a bunch. As they went out and explored new countries, they reported back that their minds changed a little bit about those countries. Perhaps the news was biased about what we should believe about those countries, and they were mostly safer and way more receptive than they were told.

In this traveling example, the couple flips the coin in their mind to see what the other side is like. This didn't remove their ability to think for themselves. It just opened them up to think about life like other people do. We, too, can exercise this mindful technique by flipping the coin in our conversations. This applies to everything. Imagine you're having a conversation or debate with someone about marijuana consumption, homelessness, or guns. They may present ideas that you disagree with. The easy thing to do is to discount them and discontinue the conversation. The more you practice flipping the coin and mulling over the opposite perspective of your own, the more likely you will be open to critical thinking and being able to see another person's perspective. And I mean see the perspective, not necessarily agree with it.

What if you practiced flipping the coin in your mind? Imagine if you try really hard to think about the same topic the way they do to understand why they think that way. You may still disagree with their results, but you might find the process intriguing because it will lead you to why they think that way. This is very much like being asked to debate another person about an issue, and you have been assigned the one side of the debate that you truly don't side with.

Sometimes, you may change your mind because you've taken the time to consider their thoughts. The idea is to be open-minded enough to listen and care. This helpful mindfulness technique gets us out of ourselves briefly and helps us consider the people around us. Of course, the perfect dovetail mindfulness technique that I spent so many years trying to convey is putting yourself in the officer's shoes. Imagine you're pulled over in a traffic stop for running a stop sign, or a police officer stops you on the street to ask you a few questions.

If the civilian in this situation would flip the coin and try to understand the primary goals and objectives of the officer, they might not be as nervous and cooperate better. Undoubtedly, the officer needs to continuously see themselves in the civilian's light. They deploy this mindfulness technique frequently in their training and on the job. If flipping the coin, the Mindfulness technique would take place at every traffic stop every time. A large majority of the misunderstandings and accidents would be avoided. Everyone would stop their emotional train wreck that could potentially happen and pause enough to consider what the other person is thinking and doing. This will allow a mental reset to happen where behaviors are checked, emotions are checked, and then actions change.

MINDFUL DRINKING

I once took a course at the University of MN that taught a variety of different mindfulness techniques like mindful walking, mindful yoga, and many others. The intentionality around being mindful of physical activities was intriguing to me. Of course, I became obsessed with the idea and tried to figure out how to use it for the people I see every day and the people I encounter in my counseling office. Practically everyone drinks or knows someone who drinks, so I feel this was a great avenue to apply mindfulness.

We all know that drinking isn't necessarily the healthiest, but if you're going to do it, I prefer you practice mindful drinking. As a preface, I'm not necessarily against drinking. If someone has a problem drinking, I always tell everyone they should get professional help. Period. Does it make you late for work? If you've been arrested for DWI, that's a problem. If anyone else in your life said you might have a problem. Then you really should look at it. If you don't have a drinking problem, I would encourage you to practice mindful drinking. Allow me to explain.

A common occurrence with drinking is someone's out with their friends and having a few beers or cocktails. They decide whether or not they're good to drive home and probably drive home anyway, regardless of their alcohol consumption. There's no parenting plan, and the inability to measure one's own alcohol consumption can be detrimental in many ways. They could get into an accident on the way home or get pulled over and get a DUI., not good outcomes.

To explain mindful drinking, I'm going to use an over the counter medication example. If you have a headache, you may try to find acetaminophen to curb the pain. You might take ibuprofen if you have inflation in your joints. Most people look at the bottle and take the prescribed amount of pills and follow the instructions, because you know if you don't, it could be bad. When you reach for that bottle of acetaminophen, you know exactly why you're using it and how much you should use. You have already predetermined the results you want to achieve by taking these pills. Your decision is calculated and measured based on the risk of taking those pills, what it could do to your body, and the relief you might feel temporarily. The same understanding should apply to our alcohol consumption.

People often self-assess their need for relaxation, avoidance, and pain relief, or to get their mind off things, and use alcohol to do it. Alcohol, and a lot of ways for people is a self-medicated avenue. The only difference between alcohol and being a coping medication strategy, is that it's not prescribed and instructed per the individual. No beer bottle will tell you how many beers you should have when you start drinking that day to achieve your affected self-medicating dose. This is where mindful drinking comes in.

There are two primary reasons why people drink alcohol. They're looking for the effects of the alcohol. One of the desired effects is that it raises impulsivity and lowers inhibitions, so that socializing with people is way more fun. They generally just want to have a good time, increase laughter, relax, and enjoy themselves.

A good example of this is people who open up a beer on Sunday when they're watching football. When football's on, they feel like they need to have a beer in their hand because that's what you do. That's what their friends are doing; therefore, they would feel awkward if they didn't do the same thing. The second basic reason people use alcohol is for stress relief. This is where they are looking for the depressant effects of the alcohol. It takes the edge off and relaxes the mind and body. In either case, much like tylenol, you wouldn't think it's healthy to use tylenol every day, and you wouldn't think it's healthy to use too much tylenol. So using alcohol mindfully similar to how you would use the medicine is considered mindful drinking.

I'm not saying use alcohol as medicine. I want to be clear there, do not use alcohol as medicine. But use it in the same emotional way. Don't have a drink because the football games are on. Measure your doses and understand why you're taking them. Also, limit how much you take based on how it affects you. Mindful drinking is pretty simple stuff, but it will change your life if you think about it that way. This practice of mindfulness can also be used for marijuana consumption, nicotine, and caffeine. Anytime we consume something that changes our mind or emotions in our mood, we should do so with mindfulness.

Mindfulness truly helps people to be more considerate and to be more understanding not only of themselves but of others. There are so many other mindfulness techniques that I would encourage you to check out, but be sure to deploy these in your life and encourage others to do the same. What harm is there in the consideration of yourself and others? Perhaps, we will slow down enough to make a mental path for others to live in our space as well. Pause your train of thought long enough to include someone else in it.

CHAPTER 10

Conclusion

IN THE MOVIE STRIPES WITH BILL MURRAY FROM 1981, a famous exchange resounds similarly to the temperament today. One of the characters, Francis Sawyer, stands up and addresses everybody in the room, saying "My name is Francis Sawyer, but everybody calls me psycho. If you call me Francis, I'll kill you.' One person mumbles back on. This caught Francis's attention, and he said "You just made the list, buddy. Also, I don't like anyone touching my stuff. So you just keep your meth hooks off. If I catch any of you guys in my stuff, I will kill you. And I don't like anybody touching me. Any of you almost touch me, and I'll kill you." Everyone looks around at the seriousness of psycho statements, and the sergeant chimes in, "Lighten up, Francis!"

It's amazing to me how this cinematic exchange correlates somewhat with the temperament today. You have a guy asking for everyone to identify him as being crazy, acting crazy, and the same person in the room speaks up and tells him to lighten up and relax. If we were to glean into the scene for a moment, we would realize that Francis was creating problems out of nothing and inflicting behavioral confrontations to soon come about. How can you have harmony with someone who doesn't allow you to call them by their name and act adversarially? It's nearly impossible.

Francis's edginess and lack of temperament control is a surefire way to explode on someone in the future. Perhaps at times, we feel like we two are confronting psychos that disguise themselves behind political lines and agendas. They'll say whatever they need to get our emotions riled up and turn us on each other. Rather than taking areas of disagreement and discussing them and debating them in civil ways, everything is taken to an absurd extreme. As Francis calls out multiple times, "I will kill you if you do anything I don't like." It sounds all too familiar today, unfortunately.

I often think of this fictional scene and conclude that the voice of reason in the sergeant is what I hope to do in my life and accomplish within this book. If we take a more patient and understanding approach and curb the extreme nature of provoking speech and actions, then perhaps we can have more harmony in our day-to-day lives. Too many of us are trapped in the persona of our political affiliations in our alliances. We are willing to kill anyone who touches those things in our emotions and our minds. It's like walking up to a house hoping to be greeted by the homeowner, but instead, he gets bit by a Rottweiler that doesn't want to let go.

Perhaps the psycho has some work to do on himself so he doesn't see the world as so jaded and can socially assimilate and be a productive member of society. If he's not able to, at least we can be. One of the first things we can Implement and encourage others to do is to curb the extremes in our minds and our beliefs. One of the primary driving forces to motivate people politically is to create an extreme situation requiring extreme emotion to respond.

If we're mindful and attentive to our thoughts and beliefs and do not allow them to become extreme, we will be more level-headed and listen to the sergeant, "Lighten up, Francis."

Every day we're presented with a reason to be frustrated, emotionally charged, and pissed off at someone who did something that should affect us. This cycle never ends. The extreme nature of getting people to rally and promote a cause never ends. I'm not saying there aren't causes worthy of promotion; I'm simply saying the process never ends. While trying to find meaning in our actions, we should relax and thoughtfully consider everyone affected by these extremes and see what role we need to play. Sometimes the person pointing the finger is the one who actually needs to change the most. Part of my hope and this resource is that everyday people can see the neutrality within the heart of the police community and what we hope to achieve alongside every civilian we encounter.

Outliers will always be there, but they should not define us. There's always a reason to magnify bias and extremes, and justify their cause, but I believe there are more reasons to side with open-mindedness and peace than overlook. The extreme nature of our media, political landscape, Hollywood, and the use of technology is deployed to get us into action.

Everybody has an agenda and tries to convince the world to partner with them. I hope that you're not only mindfully aware of the agenda they're trying to push, but that you would guard your mind and heart, than mindlessly follow someone else's agenda for your emotions and thoughts. Maybe ask yourself, should I allow this thought or emotion to run my day? How much does it actually affect me? Often times we will find out that it doesn't. We can choose not to participate in it. We can choose not to play the game of the day.

Sometimes the fear gets the better part of us, and we stop using the logical side of our brain to make decisions. It happens to everyone. Hopefully, we can learn from those times when the emotional side of our brain took over and we couldn't think clearly for ourselves. As we inch closer to understanding ourselves, we put those boundaries in place so; hopefully, it doesn't happen again, and especially so that others can't exploit this vulnerable part of us as well.

Position yourself to say no to the instant phobias of the day. We don't want to be used as some pawn and some other person's scheme to get us to turn on each other for no reason. We want to be productive members of society and help others with the ultimate dream of pursuing a life filled with liberty and happiness. Let's not sign up to be agents of divisiveness that are hell-bent on finding grudges and exploiting the mistakes and the outliers among us. Again, I'm not saying that people don't make mistakes, and I'm definitely not saying that there aren't bad people among us, including some bad cops. I am the first to demand accountability among all law enforcement officers and amongst civilians. This possible harmony and liberty is only possible with everyone following the same rules. If you treat me fair with kindness and respect, then I will do the same to you. We only start to have a problem when you're breaking the law and mistreating others, and now I have to deal with that. P.S., It might not be pleasant.

WE'RE ALL HUMAN

There's no perfect one of us out there. Everyone has flaws and is bound to make mistakes in their relationships and their profession. Based on the responsibility that we carry individually in our relationships and in our professions determines the magnitude of those mistakes and how they affect others. It just so happens that the responsibility metric for law enforcement is extraordinarily high because of the life-threatening nature of some police work. The typical person who makes mistakes at work might break the fax machine or throw away the stapler accidentally. If mistakes are made on the job of a patrolling officer, then sometimes people lose their life. That's an obvious downside to the job.

Nevertheless, it is part of the job for this life-protecting and sometimes lethal approach to commence. The reason it has been deemed necessary by the powers in charge for police officers to carry lethal and non-lethal force is to protect civilian life. Misuse and accidents are part of the equation. That is not ideal and not planned for, but I guess as long as you have humans doing the work, there's always the possibility of these unfortunate events. In the magnitude of every civilian encounter that occurs every single day on every street, hopefully, we will still see the continued benefit of every law enforcement officer and their societal roles to be understood and accepted. Sure, it would be nice if everybody followed an internal moral code and nobody had to hold anyone accountable, but that's not possible in the world we live in.

Accountability is a good thing. Accountability makes us better because we hold people to a higher standard. A standard that says your life is important, and we as a society are willing to set up a scenario in which you have personal freedoms. You can express yourself within those passions and desires that you have in life to be happy and to have a family. You are willing to hold people accountable around you that might infringe on your liberties and prevent and punish those that desire to steal, kill and destroy those freedoms that you have. That's why accountability is beautiful because our freedoms are valuable. If we don't care to have accountability, how much do we value our freedoms and life?

MY PLEA

This is my plea to disincentivize politicians for using law enforcement as some political tool. I hope that through this book and others like it, you, too, will concur that law enforcement and our personal freedoms shouldn't ever be some ploy used as a political maneuver. We may always have politics that bring tremendous divisiveness. Still, we are unwilling to allow others to play with our freedoms and the institutions that protect them to try to persuade and win an argument. Our life and our liberty are too valuable to be played with.

Law enforcement is not about promoting racism, brutality, aggression, or mistreatment of others. We are about ensuring the place where the laws of the land are abided by and there's a desire to prevent and pursue people who choose to mistreat others and mistreat themselves. We don't sign for it or agree to it; that is not who we are. If you are not a fan of accountability, go live elsewhere. If you're not a fan of abiding by the laws of the land, go live elsewhere because here, we have standards. We won't let those that don't care very much for themselves and their environment, dictate our land's standards. We care too much about our communities, relationships, and belongings to let criminals take precedence over what is permissible. We will not stoop down to the lowest standard of care and allow those with no accountability, responsibility, or personal ambition to lead us in our way of life. So as we continue to recognize the law for authority in the land, we realize the need for them and our appreciation for who they are because they protect what we care so much about. If we don't care to have any personal freedoms, belonging, or peace in our land, then let us do away with this lawful authority. If we are to keep them around, let us empower them to do their job and understand the tremendous sacrifice they provide for us daily. We all know that they're not doing it for money!

Contention in society leads to a rise in crime, where it costs everybody financially and emotionally. Is that what we truly want? Don't we want to raise our kids with acceptance and love in their hearts rather than convince them that they're supposed to be in opposition to their neighbor because they may have different thoughts in their mind or because they may have a different skin color? We don't have to agree to it. We don't have to be part of the game that's being played. Let's raise our kids differently and show kindness to our neighbors.

MY HOPE

Most of today's community problems can be solved civilly and responsibly with a local approach and a social connection that promotes de-escalation and open dialogue. When people meet face to face and discuss their thoughts and their fears, often, the logical side of the brain picks up on our human traits, and we assess the problems of our day with a little bit more compassion and a little bit more understanding. When we're presented with the idea that we're supposed to turn on our neighbor, we reject it wholeheartedly, so it's no longer a tool used against us. We combat societal and political aggression with logic and reason. We can count the facts and wait patiently for them to present themselves rather than acting irrationally and responsively when our emotions get triggered.

I hope you'll become the hope for change in your family and community. We can bring positive solutions that advance life's processes that lead us to better outcomes versus approaches that are detrimental in the short term and long term. We're better together and more productive when we work together to pursue life, liberty, and happiness. Thank you for being a part of the solution and for being a productive member of society because your life is being broadcasted to everyone around you as the standard for their life. You can make a difference by becoming the best version of yourself.

Thank you so much for picking up my book and making it this far. It means that you care for yourself, your community, law enforcement, and our nation. I appreciate you taking the time and processing these deep and emotional things with me. Hopefully, we can make a difference together in this beautiful place we call home.